1⁵⁰⁰

MW01141994

FOOTSTEPS OF FAITH
...living our faith in everyday life.

by Jeanne Cook

Copyright © 2013 by Jeanne Cook
Vida Ministries
PO Box 6433
Lafayette, IN 47903-6433

ISBN: 978-1-304-01291-3

Published by Vida Ministries. Cover design by Patrick Caulley.

TABLE OF CONTENTS

PREFACE

I have always loved to write, so when the Lord told me to start journaling it came very easy for me. It helped in so many ways to work through my emotions and stress. It was like medicine to my soul as I wrote about the hardships and joys that had consumed my life.

The Lord then asked me to write a book about all of our experiences. As I re-read my journals, I cried and cried as I saw God's special grace on our lives.

We were asked to begin teaching classes in the missions program at Rhema Bible Training Center. It was in those classes that I realized the need and importance to encourage young people to follow after God's plan for their lives. God's compassion for the people always comes before He sends you there. If that is not there upon arrival, then it is not the direction that He has for you.

We began hosting interns from different Bible schools, introducing them to the reality of life on the mission field. Our greatest passion for those interns is to invest our lives into them and encourage them to follow God's plan for their lives.

As you read this book, my desire is for you to see how faithful God is to protect and provide for you as you dare to leap out in His plan for your life. I promise you that your greatest joy in life is walking in His divine plan.

My personal email is jeanne.vidamin@gmail.com.

Jeanne Cook

CHAPTER ONE
"LORD, IF YOU WILL RADICALLY SAVE DENNIS, I WILL GO ANYWHERE AND DO ANYTHING."

I was raised in a Christian home, and as far as I can remember I always had a real deep love for God. He was always the most important thing in my life. I had a very good upbringing and my parents taught me to honor God in everything I did and to consider Him in all my ways and decisions in life.

IN THE BEGINNING

Most of my upbringing was in Kokomo, Indiana. Indiana is basically all farm area. At that time there were not many industries or jobs outside of farming. I lived on a farm for many years. My father loved farming, and he put that love into all of his children. There were two automobile factories in the small town of Kokomo: Delco Remy and the Chrysler Corporation. They assembled parts for the main factories that were located in other larger cities. These two factories employed about 40% of the population in our area.

Most of the people farmed even if they worked in the factories. The factories paid well and their benefits were outstanding. It was a dream to get hired on there. For the farmers, it helped them pay off their large farming equipment bills.

Indiana is a beautiful state. The lands are all open fields used for farming. I love all of the seasons of the year there.

In spring you began plowing the fields in order to plant the next month. It was always so fascinating to me to see the little sprouts come up each year. The fields would be full and bring forth such a large harvest that you could not see much outside of your own back yard.

The summer months were work months. The vegetables had to be canned and put away for winter. We worked the fields with our parents and siblings. On Saturdays we always went to town and sold our vegetables from house to house. This was a very profitable business. We also had a vegetable stand that we maintained throughout the week.

FOOTSTEPS OF FAITH

As a child we would lie on our backs and try to find the Big Dipper in the evenings. We would lie there for hours until bedtime each night talking and watching the wonders of the sky.

At the end of summer when we had already harvested the crops, the tractors would cut down the leftover corn husks and make them into bales of hay to feed the livestock during the winter months. During this time the fields were barren and you could see for miles once again.

Soon after the summer season is over the fall season begins. The fall is beautiful in Indiana. All the leaves on the trees turn different colors of yellow and brown and fall to the ground.

As children we would play in the fallen leaves for hours. In those days no one raked the leaves from their yards. They used the leaves to replenish the natural resources of the earth. They believed it was good for the soil to let the leaves go back into the earth. I think it is what we call "mulch" today.

Then the cold winds of winter would brush across the fields. It gets very cold in winter in Indiana and there are a lot of snowy days. Most of our fields became ice-skating rinks during the winter months. As soon as school was out each day we headed for the ice to practice our ice-skating skills. It was a lot of fun.

Most farmers lived miles apart so it was rare to have visitors. Families were very close. As a family you did everything together. Family members were your best and closest friends.

I was raised Catholic and always went to Catholic schools. When I became of age to go to high school my parents did not want to send me away to boarding school, so they sent me to the only public school in our town.

That is where I met Dennis Cook, the love of my life. We began dating and fell in love. I remember the reason he stood out to me over all of the other guys in school. He was a very sincere person. He was very honest and I always felt secure that what he told me he really meant. There was no playing games with him. On our third date he told me that he was in love with me. I told him that was ridiculous; no one could fall in love that quickly! He said that he had loved me since the sixth grade. I was a cheerleader and our paths had crossed, and I did not even know it.

We dated through high school and got married right after I graduated. Dennis joined the Air Force and his first assignment was to Karamürsel, Turkey. His tour of duty was for 18 months. He was a private. When you are low-ranking, the government did not pay for your spouse to accompany you. We had to save our money to buy my ticket to join him.

We were apart for nine months. During part of this time I worked for a local clothing store in our hometown. I lived with my parents until I was able to save enough money to go with Dennis. My job was very good experience for me. They taught all of their employees how to do the ordering of clothing and makeup. They taught us how to decorate the show windows in front of the store. We were obligated to model all of the clothing in the store and to wear it while we worked there. It was good experience, but it did not pay very well.

The local factory called me and I went to work there. They paid very well, and in no time I had enough money to purchase my ticket to go be with Dennis.

LIFE IN TURKEY

I had never been away from home so that was a great challenge for me. I had never flown before and the trip was 14 hours in the air. I was 19 years old. When I arrived I quickly made up my mind that everything was going to be all right now that Dennis was with me.

Dennis did not have enough rank to live on base, so we lived on the Turkish economy. We rented a small apartment in a two-story house in a little town named Karamürsel, one

hour by bus to the American military base where Dennis worked. The landlord lived upstairs. He was a doctor by profession. The house was located one block from the Black Sea. The winters were very cold and the summers always had a nice breeze that came off of the sea. The countryside was green and very beautiful.

The country of Turkey was fascinating to me. I love different cultures and ways of life. I was a history buff in school, and Turkey was full of history. I wanted to visit all the famous mosques and landmarks on Dennis's time off from work.

Istanbul is really something to see. Inside each mosque the dome was painted by a famous artist. The Blue Mosque was my favorite. I wanted to spend days there lying on my back studying each little detail of the art on the ceiling. It was one of those experiences that make an impression on your life forever.

Istanbul also had an open market where people from different countries would come and sell their wares. It was a dangerous place to go because of Dennis's job in the Air Force. We were heavily guarded everywhere we went. Dennis had top security clearance and he was targeted to be kidnapped. Secret Service men know things that could really put the safety of the United States at risk, so the Air Force tried their best to make sure all of the top Secret Service people and their families were safe.

The open market had all kinds of people there, mostly of the Moslem religion. They were not dark people like I had imagined; they were an ash color. They had sable brown hair and very beautiful black eyes. The men all wore Turkish large-legged pants that draped around their waist and large turbans on their heads. The men sat around in chai houses all day drinking chai tea which is a very strong tea. It was heavily sugared.

The women covered their faces and wore long black dresses that covered every part of their body. You never saw a woman in public uncovered. Although you could only see their eyes through their veils, you could pretty well read their lives through their eyes. Turkish people do not value their women very highly.

Early every morning before the sun came up a town crier would get on a loud speaker and call everyone to prayer. You could hear it all over Turkey. Each city had a town crier. At noon the same thing would happen and at 6 p.m. each evening. It did not matter where they were or what they were doing. They fell to their knees, doubled over their bodies so their faces touched the pavement, and began to chant rehearsed prayers. In their culture when you bow to the pavement you are in complete surrender to your god. Even the children in school practiced this form of worship. If you were not Moslem, you had to stand quietly during this time to show respect for the culture that you were in.

It was not a friendly country towards the United States. They would spit on the ground when an American walked by.

There was relatively little or almost no crime in Turkey. The punishment for crime was very high so it really discouraged it. If a man was caught stealing, they cut off his hands that took the merchandise and his legs so he could not run away from the scene of the crime.

Because Dennis was in Secret Service in the Air Force he was on call 24 hours a day. Sometimes the base commander's wife would call me and say, "There is a red alert on base. I do not know when your husband will be home." Dennis was a code detector on the radio. His job was to record and keep track of all the communications within the country's radios. They would always talk in code so he also worked on decoding their secret codes. He loved his job and was quickly promoted. Dennis's father was a career man in the Army so it came natural to Dennis to love the service life.

Because I was alone so much, the landlord's wife adopted me. Every day she would come down to get me and we would go up to her apartment to fellowship. The apartment was full of other women who were all related one way or another. It was common for many families to live in the same apartment. The women spoke English fluently. They were an upper-class family who did not have the same opinion that the regular Turkish people had about Americans. A lot of them studied in the United States. I ate lunch every day with them. Their food was very greasy and seasoned with curry.

The Turkish people had many customs that were very different than the United States. For one thing the woman was mainly an instrument used to reproduce. When a woman would get pregnant she was not allowed to go out in public. After the baby was born she remained in the house until the baby was 6 months old. Then they could both go out in public. They nursed their children until they were 5 years old and went to school. Girls were not given the same opportunities to excel like boys. There were very few educated women when we lived there.

The Turkish people did not believe in eating beef or pork. The cow was sacred along with the cat. They believed the next ruler of Turkey would be bitten on the heel by a cat. Most of their shoes had no back to them so the cats would have an opportunity to bite them. The cats there were as large as a small dog. The only meat you saw hanging in the fly-infested shops was lamb and goat. They drank goat milk and ate goat cheese.

I learned a lot about people and different cultures by living in Turkey. I learned to respect each culture and not to think we were superior in everything because we were Americans.

BACK ON AMERICAN SOIL

I became pregnant with our first child in Turkey. I stayed there with Dennis until my seventh month of pregnancy. I flew home to have our first baby. There were no hospitals in Karamürsel, so you had to fly to Ankara to have your baby. There was only one flight a week. If you had your baby early, you had to give birth alone. I was not brave enough to do that, so I flew home to my mother's house in America to have the baby.

We named our first son Christopher Scott. He was born on January 28, 1969, at Grissom Air Force Base in Bunker Hill, Indiana.

After we returned from our overseas assignment we were

stationed at Lackland Air Force Base in San Antonio, Texas, and lived in base housing.

Our second child was born there on February 1, 1970. We named her Jennifer Renee.

Dennis began going to college in San Antonio, Texas. The Air Force and school consumed most of Dennis's time. He was very ambitious and wanted to make a difference in this world. He loved education like his father. Dennis was the only one of five children that loved education like his father. His father had many degrees and after he retired from the Army he taught in their schools for years. He was a very brilliant man.

After our term in the Air Force was over we moved back to our home town. Dennis went back to work and we bought a little two-bedroom bungalow home on Purdum Street. It was our first home. We were so proud of it.

Dennis returned to his old job at the Delco Remy automobile factory. He worked sometimes sixty hours a week and went to college in the evenings. He went full time so it was very time-consuming. He majored in the medical field. He knew he wanted to be a doctor, but he did not know what area he wanted to specialize in.

On November 11, 1971, our third child was born. We named him Jason.

Then on April 26, 1973, our fourth child was born. We named him Chad Ryan.

We had four children in five years. I was 24 years old by this time.

DENNIS

Education became the passion of Dennis's life. He lost all track of God in his life. I was at home 24 hours a day with four small children under 5 years old. It was during this season of my life that I cried out to the Lord and promised Him that, if he would radically save Dennis, I would go anywhere and be willing to do anything.

Dennis was no longer a part of our lives and his children did not know him.

Dennis has a brilliant mind like his father. He has a photographic memory, so once he reads something, he knows it for life. He was very intellectual and loved to debate about everything. He was in his sixth year of pre-med. His grades were very high. In six years of college he made mostly all A's and one C. The C was in calculus. That one C robbed him of the joy of all the A's he had made.

He was a bookworm and hated the outdoors. Almost nothing made him happy in life. He was probably the most unsatisfied person

that I had ever known. He was an extreme introvert and could not find happiness anywhere or in anything. He would set goals, yet when he achieved them, he found no fulfillment. He had a huge void inside and could not fill it. When he found the Lord, that void was filled.

Six months after I prayed that prayer, Dennis got radically born again. Chad was 2 years old, Jason was 3, Jennifer was almost 4 and Chris was 5.

This picture was taken when Dennis got born again. Up to that time it was our only family picture.

Dennis was everything to us now. He had come back into our lives and we were his whole world. Nothing could touch my heart so deeply as that. I was willing to go anywhere God would send us for what He had done for me.

Dennis became an extrovert. Now he is very outgoing and everything is so exciting to him. He loves life and everything in it. As long as we go with him, he is willing to go anywhere for the Lord. He loves people and likes to spend hours talking to them.

He was wild and crazy and loved the word "impossible." If someone said it was impossible, Dennis was going to be the one that proved it was possible.

He lost all interest in education. Although he had 13 years of seniority and full medical benefits, Dennis quit his job and put our sweet little bungalow up for sale. He dropped out of college and said he wanted to go into the ministry. Our house sold in three days. I do not think we even listed it in the paper. Our parents were in shock. They, as well as I, thought we would live there forever. We had the only grandchildren on both sides of my family so that was a huge factor for my parents.

The fact that I was leaving the Catholic church created a distance between us. This was very hard for me because I was daddy's little girl. My sun rose and sat in my daddy. His rejection was very hard on me. The Lord spoke to me very clearly the scripture in Matthew 10:37 that says:

> *He that loveth father or mother more than me is not*
> *worthy of me: and he that loveth son or daughter more*
> *than me is not worthy of me.*

I had to put the call of God on my life before my love for my parents. How could I say no to God after He had kept His word to me? I just had to keep my part of the promise. So I made a decision to keep my word and trust God to work it out with my parents. He was so faithful to do that.

Dennis's mom and dad were divorced. His mom remarried and so did his father. His mom lived in our hometown but his father lived in South Carolina. His mother had two other grandchildren that were older than ours. His father had two stepchildren with his new wife plus the three that were with Dennis's mother.

BIBLE SCHOOL

We moved to Tulsa, Oklahoma, and went to Rhema Bible Training Center. The children were ages 4 through 8 when we moved. When Chad started kindergarten I started Bible school with Dennis. It was in Bible school that God birthed in me a cry for the nations. Bible school changed my life. It sure broadened my world. It made me love God even more deeply than I did before. I was willing to do anything to serve Him. I had such a hunger inside for a deeper revelation of God. I wanted to serve Him with my life more than anything in this world. I had tasted the other life and found that it did not matter to me where the call on our lives took us. As long as I was with Dennis and our children, I would be perfectly happy. There is just something about being in the divine will of God that makes all of the difference in the world. There is a special grace there to help you make all of the changes necessary to adapt. You can live in the worst of conditions but yet be happy as a lark.

Every time a missionary came to school we would sit and cry through the whole class. During this time Dennis took his first missions trip. He went to Quetzaltenango, Guatemala. It was there that the Lord told him in 14 months we would be on the mission field.

During Bible school Dennis had a vision of a man getting on an airplane. The airplane landed in a leper colony. The man preached the gospel and many were born again and healed in their bodies. Dennis prayed and prayed for that leper colony but had no idea that he was the man who would be sent there.

After graduation we moved back to our hometown and worked with Dennis's brother who was a pastor. They had established a church together in Kokomo before we left to go to Bible school. We worked with him for about 10 months.

The Lord told Dennis to leave our home country for Panama, Central America, by the end of November 1981. He then told him that he was the man in the vision. Dennis was so shocked! When he first shared the vision with me, I had known he was the man in the vision, but I did not say anything. I know how important it is for the man to get the direction.

The Lord told Dennis that we would walk into a work already established. He said we would be a member of a large Spanish-speaking church, plus minister to the American military. At that time the United States had 10 American bases in Panama. They were established to guard the Panama Canal. This was where we would begin our mission journey.

GOODBYE

The middle of November we had a moving sale to get rid of all of our belongings. This is the time I realized what I was doing. We had an open house and all our friends came to say goodbye to us. My parents couldn't bring themselves to come because it was just too painful.

I went around and priced all of the memories of my life for the past 12 years. There was Chris's little wooden rocking horse and all of Chad's and Jason's little trucks that had been handed down from Chris.

All their little things were really nothing, but each had a very special memory in their hearts. I gave each child a large suitcase and watched them as they packed their favorite toys and things.

I watched Chris pack his teddy bear that he had gotten for his first birthday. It played music then but no longer worked. He had rubbed all the hair off of it so it was hairless. In the back there was a patch where the bear got hurt and we had to patch him up. There really was not much left of the bear, but he wanted to take that bear with him, so we did. Chris also loved to read, so he took some books.

Chad packed all his trucks. He had just about every Fisher Price truck and the action figures to go along with the theme of the truck. He packed the ambulance truck, the Special Forces truck and, slowly but surely, his suitcase was full. Then at the last moment he said, "Oh, I almost forgot Joey." Joey was a Fisher Price doll that Chad learned to button buttons and tie his shoes on. Joey was missing an arm because the dog tried to take it away from Chad and somehow the dog ended up with the arm. He even packed Joey's arm in case we could figure out how to put it back on someday.

Jason packed the funniest things. Some of them were trucks and mostly his favorite homemade things like paper airplanes and rockets and things that he had made in school.

Jennifer packed some of her dolls, mostly the Barbie dolls. Jennifer loved books, and still does, so her suitcase was mainly full of books.

Everything they chose held a very special place in their little hearts. The hardest thing for me to watch being sold was Jennifer's doll house. Dennis had built her a five-foot-tall doll house for her Barbie dolls after he got saved. He furnished it with everything, and Jennifer played nonstop with that doll house for about two years. We even moved it to Oklahoma when we went to Bible school.

After that day I felt as if my whole heart had been ripped out. I was so insecure about what we were doing. This was totally not like me to agree to something so wild. I like everything in order before I make a move. We were flying by the seat of our pants with no preparation. I was not comfortable with it at all, but Dennis was out-of-his-mind happy. He was wild and invincible. He assured me everything was in God's hands and we would be just fine.

THE JOURNEY BEGINS...PANAMA

We took Dennis's niece Kathy with us. She felt a call of God to the Spanish-speaking countries. She spoke Spanish, so that was such a blessing.

Our good friends Pastor Tennyson and Carol Fitch prayed for us and sent us out.

When we arrived the night of

November 30, 1981, we did not know one person. The night sky was lit up with street lights. I was so scared but yet so excited! I wondered why God would send us to this country so far away. There must have been a person praying that He would send someone. It simply amazes me how God listens to our cries. The Bible tells us that He loves His children so much that He knows how many hairs are on each of our heads. Medical science tells us that no two people have the same iris, finger print, or voice. He knows every one of us by name and, when we cry out to Him, He knows exactly who is crying by the tone of our voice. I love that about Him.

We spent the night in the Holiday Inn that was close to the airport. I think it was the only hotel in Panama at that time. The next day we rented a car to spy out the land. The city was really big compared to Kokomo. It was not very modern and the society seemed so laid back. It was such a change from our fast-paced society in America. Every day at noon the people would go home for lunch and a siesta, returning to work at 3 p.m. Then at 5 p.m. everything, including gas stations and grocery stores, shut down in Panama.

The Latin women are very pretty. The men are everything my mother told me to stay away from. Most have dark hair and dark eyes. They were very persuasive and used a lot of flattery.

There were all kinds of people in Panama City because of the Panama Canal. I would say that all nations were represented there. Most people had come through the Panama Canal, fell in love with it, and just stayed.

We were fascinated by the huge ships that went through the Canal. The logistics of how something that large could be navigated through such a small passage fascinated all of us. Panama is located between two oceans, the Pacific and the Atlantic. It is absolutely beautiful.

I was overtaken by the massiveness of the ocean. It seemed like there was no end to it. It reminded me of the grace and mercy of God and how endless His love is towards us. I loved the ocean and found it to be medicine to my soul.

I could have spent all day there just enjoying the ocean. My heart wanted to fall down and worship God. We were on such new ground and everything in my life had changed. I felt very insecure. The only thing that never changes in your life is God. He is always the same. His Word will always hold your world together. No matter what happened, we knew we could always cry out to Jesus and He would be right there to help us. His name holds all of the power in the entire universe. There is absolutely nothing that is more powerful than His name. So that day I hid myself and all of my fears under the shadow of the Almighty. I told Him that I would keep my word to Him no matter how hard it got. I do not know what happened to me in that moment of time, but it seemed like grace was imparted to me for the call on our lives. I knew that I had to be strong for the children. Children react to things according to the way they are presented to them. If they think you are insecure, then they become insecure.

I knew that it was very important for Dennis to feel like I was 100% behind him. I told God that day that I would never stand in the way of the call on Dennis's life. I knew he was called to do something really big for God. I did not want my insecurities to be a hindrance to him. I wanted him to know that I was with him through it all. This was already too big for me to shoulder in my own strength so I decided to just cling really tight to the Lord's hand and to turn Dennis loose to be everything that he was called to be.

Dennis called his brother that night, and his brother told us to contact José Silva, the head of the television program "Praise the Lord" in Central America. José invited us to his office the next day. As we began sharing our hearts with him, he told his secretary to cancel all of his meetings for that day. He patiently listened for hours as we told how faithful God had been to us and how we were putting all of our confidence in Him. I know his heart went out to us because we had four little kids and just wanted to do God's will in our lives. He spent the whole afternoon with us. Then he said, "If you can be here tomorrow morning, I have someone that I want you to meet."

So the next morning we went to his office and he introduced us to David Spencer. David Spencer and his father had pioneered all of the underground churches in Nicaragua. He invited us over to his place for breakfast. As we shared with him what God had put on our hearts, he began to smile. He said, "Let's worship God, and see what His plan is here." We must have worshipped together an hour. David played the piano and sang like he was born to worship God. He began to tell us his vision. God had sent him there to open a Spanish-speaking church. He had been believing God for an American couple to come and start an English service in his church. It was right in the heart of an American military base. He fasted and prayed at the leper colony every month. He had been going there for years.

David's parents lived in an apartment on top of David's house but they were on furlough. The apartment was fully furnished, which was a blessing since we had nothing but our clothing and favorite trucks and dolls with us. He offered it to us for $350 a month. We were only getting $350 a month support, but we took a step of faith and rented it.

David told us that he had sent for three couples to come to do this work. All three backed out. He knew the Lord had told him to begin it, but in the natural it was just not coming together.

You just never know what God has in mind. Who would have thought He would call a man thousands of miles away and give such detailed information as to where and what he would be doing. David said he knew it was God when we began to share all of the details. It was too detailed to be coincidental.

That next day David went with us and helped us to begin the work for the Lord. David was a great person to work for. He had millions of stories that would keep you captivated for hours. He was very wild and loved living on the edge like Dennis did, and still does. It was a bit scary when they were together because you never knew where they would end up!

So the next week we moved into the apartment. We had never lived with all four children in an apartment before. It was interesting with four children plus Dennis's niece Kathy. She was 18 years old and a tremendous help to us in every way.

We began visiting the American military families. We went house to house and invited them to church. We visited them once a week and got to know many of them very well. Most of them were on their first overseas tour and were far away from home. We certainly could relate to them, remembering our tour in Turkey.

THE BEGINNING OF MIRACLES

While pastoring that little church we saw many miracles.

FOOTSTEPS OF FAITH

One day our children were playing outside, building a birdhouse. They decided to climb a huge tree and put the birdhouse on the farthest limb. A little girl who was with them decided she would be the one to crawl out on the limb. When she did she fell about 40 feet to the ground. The kids came running upstairs and told us that the little girl had fallen. When Dennis got there she was lying on her back. He took her pulse and she had none. Her eyes were rolled back into her head. There was no life in her anywhere.

The Spirit of the Lord fell on Dennis and his heart began to break with compassion for this little girl. He covered her with his body and said he felt the life of him go out into the little girl's body. He began to pray and groan in the spirit in other tongues. About that time her parents came running out of the house. There was life transferred into the little girl's body. She began to groan in pain. Her eyes became dilated and her heart began to beat once again. She had been dead for about ten minutes, if I remember right. Her father hysterically took the little girl up into his arms and they rushed her to the hospital. They called us from the hospital and said that she was in bad condition. They said she had a severe head injury, her arm was broken, she had bruised kidneys and many other serious injuries.

When the mother told me what the medical report was, it was like the spirit of faith came all over me. I said to her, "No, when the Lord heals, He heals completely!" Her mother had them run the test again and found she did have a concussion but nothing serious. Her arm was not broken. She did not have bruised kidneys or any other serious injuries. She was bruised badly and very sore.

They kept her a couple of days to observe her. When they sent her home, she told of how she was in heaven with Jesus. She heard Dennis praying. The Lord told her she could not stay because the prayer of faith had been prayed for her. Then He told her that her mission on this earth was not completed and that she would have to go back and complete that mission because it was too early to come home.

I cannot explain to you the tremendous amount of compassion that overtakes you when something happens like that. I have seen nine people raised from the dead and that compassion was always present. Afterwards everyone cries and cries because of the goodness of the Father. That He would reach out of heaven and touch their loved one birthed such an appreciation in their lives for His goodness and His love towards mankind.

In our small little church there was a couple, Junior and Alicia Rivera, that will always hold a very dear place in our hearts. I don't think they had any idea that their tithes were what we fed our family on. Junior was a mechanic on the large airplanes that flew into the bases.

One time they said they had a special gift for us. They bought us a car! This was a couple that did not own a car themselves yet they sacrificed and bought us one. Their lives touched our lives so deeply.

During this time a man moved to Panama from Lakewood Church, Pastor John Osteen's church in Houston, Texas. He said that the Lord told him to come to Panama and dig for gold. He joined a church close to where he was staying. It happened to be an Assembly of God church not too far off of the American base where we lived.

The pastor of that church had kind of given up on miracles and signs and wonders. He believed in them but had not seen them for years in his church. The pastor said, "I will believe it when I see it." No one believed that God would show a man where the gold was in the earth. The man boldly said, "If I hit a large vein of gold, will you go with me to John Osteen's church and have him pray for your heart?" The pastor needed open heart surgery at the time. So the pastor said, "It's a deal!" When the man hit the largest vein of gold ever hit in Panama, the pastor kept his end of the deal. He went with him to be prayed for and was healed!

We saw many miraculous things while we pastored that small church. It holds a special place in our hearts. It was awesome to see the plan of God unfold in our lives. We pastored the little church for 18 months.

THE LEPER COLONY

Once David Spencer took us to visit the leper colony. We had to walk because we did not have a car yet. It was five miles from where we lived. All the kids went with us. I remember the road was very overgrown and it looked like no one cared about anything there. My heart began to cry as I realized that these people had been ostracized from society. No one cared if they lived or died. When we finally arrived, Dennis stood back and just stared in amazement for such a long time. He said it was just like what he had seen in the vision. He took my hand and held it so tight as if to say that we were about to step

into the ministry that God had moved us across the continent for. With his hand in mine, I knew everything was going to be all right.

The colony itself was fairly large. It had a very weatherworn sign that was partially torn down. It read "Palo Seco Leper Colony." Palo seco means "dried up tree." The colony was roughly painted with a blue paint that looked like leftover paint no one wanted. There was not enough to cover the whole complex so they just painted what they could.

The colony had windows all around it and a wheelchair ramp, since most of the residents were confined to wheelchairs. It faced the ocean with a very beautiful view. I remember seeing a man collecting shells out there. We later met him and got to be very good friends with him. He was the gardener at the leper colony. He did not have leprosy. He planted all kinds of beautiful flowers and trees around the colony for the people to enjoy. His name was Lester.

The first room that they took us to was the largest room. It had about 20 beds in it. I will never forget my first impression of the people with this horrible disease. Some had no eyeballs, no legs, and no nose. Most had something missing on their body.

One thing that greatly impressed me was how they loved one another. Later I realized that it was the only family they had ever known. Most of them left their homes when they were young and had never left the leper colony. My heart cried for their souls, and Dennis's vision soon became the passion of my heart as well. It is amazing to me that it did not matter that these people were not whole. It was like I did not see how horrible the disease had eaten away at their bodies.

Someone had given us a bunch of hand-cranked tape recorders

with Bible cassettes to give to the people. We raised enough money to be able to purchase some tape recorders and a complete set of Bible tapes for each person.

Juan was the first person we were introduced to. He was very intelligent but was missing both eyeballs. Juan liked to talk for hours about places he had visited before they diagnosed him with leprosy. Dennis loved to talk so he would sit for hours talking to Juan.

Then there was Yeaya. She looked to be about 70 years old. She no longer could walk so she stayed in the wheelchair and looked out at the ocean all day. Sometimes the nurses would take the patients to visit each other.

Yeaya told us that she came to the colony when she was just 9 years old. Our son Jason was 9 at that time. Yeaya told of the day her parents sent her away. They took all record of her off of their family history. They were ashamed that they had a daughter who had leprosy. Her birth certificate and shot records, everything, were burned as they sent her away. She looked back as the boat took her away. She knew that she would never see her family again. Her family had never visited her or contacted her since then.

Yeaya was full of so many stories about the leper colony and what it used to look like. Chad and Jason loved to listen to her, and she loved the attention of small children. She said when she came to the colony everyone lived in caves and only came out at night because the light hurt their eyes. The government fed them once a day, and they just threw the food out in front of the caves because no one wanted to get near them. They were cursed by God and man rejected them. She said no one bathed or was taken care of. There was no medicine or any help whatsoever.

One day Yeaya was talking to Chad who was 9 years old by that time. Chad asked Yeaya if she had ever married. She told him no, but she always wanted to be. He asked her if she ever wanted a little boy. She said, "Oh, yes, I have always wanted a little boy." He said, "Well, when I left Indiana I left my grandma and I am very lonely for her. If you will be my grandma then I will be your little boy." Yeaya cried and cried, and accepted his offer.

Chad would get in her wheelchair with her and spend hours talking to her. He would rub her face and kiss her hands. It was so sweet watching him with his new grandma.

Rafael, another member of the leper colony, was very dear to my heart. He sat all day looking out at orchids in his front yard. He loved

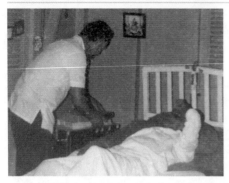

orchids. Lester had planted Rafael's small yard full of different kinds of orchids. I remember he asked us to be there on one very special day. We had no idea what was going on but we went. When we got there he showed us an orchid that only blooms once a year. It had bloomed that morning. How he calculated the time it would bloom I have no idea. It was wonderful sharing that special moment in his life.

Luis and his wife lived in the leper colony. Luis did not have leprosy but his wife did. Luis had a very bad heart. He was the first person that would let us pray for him. He needed open heart surgery. Dennis prayed for him. When he went to the doctor, the doctor told him that he had a new heart!

This opened the door for us to start praying for others in the colony. They would never let you pray for their leprosy because they knew if they got healed they would have to leave the colony and it was the only home they had ever known.

We began going into the colony once a week. The people would spend the longest time thanking us for visiting them. I know our children were the only children that they had seen in years. They absolutely loved to just watch them and talk to them. It was the highlight of their lives.

We spent two years teaching in the leper colony. We visited the colony once a week and taught in the church that had been abandoned in the colony. Dennis would teach about two hours every time we went, but then we spent the whole day with the lepers talking and just befriending them. Most of them had been taught that they had leprosy because God had put a curse on them. Dennis taught on the character of God for two years.

Lester would never come to the services but would stand outside listening to what Dennis was teaching. One day we went to the colony and Lester was not there. Our children were disappointed because Lester would take them shelling in the ocean. They loved Lester and he loved them. When we asked where he was, they said they put him into the hospital because they found leprosy in both of his feet.

The next time we went back, Lester was at the gate waiting on us. He said, "You know, Dennis, what you teach here saved my life." Dennis said, "What do you mean?" Lester said, "Well, when they told me that I had leprosy in both of my feet, your words kept ringing in my ears. 'God is a good God. He died on the cross for our sins and infirmities.' So I  said to God, 'If this is true, what Dennis preaches, I am asking You to heal my feet of leprosy.'" The next morning he was scheduled to have both of his feet amputated. When the doctors examined his feet, they were amazed. They decided to take the entire test again and found no leprosy in any part of his feet or body. He was totally healed!

When Lester was healed the people began to ask us to pray for their illnesses. None would ask to have the leprosy healed. They wanted to live in the colony for the rest of their lives.

During this time there was a scientist who started doing research on leprosy. He found that the armadillos that lived around the colony had contracted leprosy. He began to study them and came to the medical knowledge that this disease came from a bacteria called Mycobacterium leprae and could be treated like the common cold. It was contagious through the liquids of the body. The reason the people had missing limbs was because leprosy affected the nervous system. They could not feel their arms and legs, so at night the rats would eat them.

As time progressed they built a hospital and began taking care of the people. They were given medicine, bathed regularly and well-taken care of. Everything changed once the doctor found out how to treat leprosy. Before that, the only way they knew to treat it was to cut off what had been infected.

Many organizations began sending in aid and people to care for the people with leprosy. Many churches began coming in, too, and preaching on a regular basis. We worked with them all in helping the progress of the colony.

During this time we were pastoring our English-speaking church. The church was going well and was really growing. Dennis started two Bible studies on the American military bases. There were ten American military bases located in Panama at this time. I believe they estimated that there were 10,000 military families living in Panama then.

OUR CHURCH AND BIBLE STUDIES

God gave us a lot of favor with some pretty high-up people in the military. One of the Bible studies was held on a small naval base in Panama called Amador. In this study was the man who would become the head of the Panama Canal Commission. You just never know who God will put in your path! This man had a real impact on all of the people in the Panama Canal Commission. He was a Christian in every area of his life, and he radiated the love of the Father.

Another Bible study was held on Fort Clayton in a colonel's home. We worked with the base chaplains and began a joint effort in reaching the lost. At this time we helped bring a lot of unity among the different denominations with a movement called Corsillo. It was very successful, and many people's lives were totally changed by that movement in Panama.

Then I began to have a Bible study on Fort Clayton which was in a mixed dormitory. That was an eye-opener for me.

We were very involved with the American military families. Dennis's father was a lifer and the military life had a special place in Dennis's life. We made a lot of good friends during this time and are still close to these people after all these years on the mission field.

We began a Bible study at Fort Amador in the home of Larry and Shirley Madkins. A lot of career officers belonged to that Bible study. Chaplain Harry and Marlynn Brown participated in that study. We got to be very close friends with them.

We began another Bible study in the home of Colonel John and Sandy Walters. It was such a blessing to us to get to know a lot of the people at Fort Clayton.

THE NEXT STEP

The head of the organization that David Spencer was under told him that his English-speaking service was too close to another of their English churches. They told

him to close it down.
So our church was
gone. David felt really
bad, but convinced us
that God was about
to do something new
in our lives. So he
invited us to go to a
ministers' luncheon.
It was very nice and
we met some really
incredible pastors.

One pastor kept staring at us all through the luncheon. It made me very uncomfortable. Afterwards he came up to us and asked forgiveness for being so rude by staring all through the luncheon.

He said that he was just in shock when he saw us. He then began telling us that he had a vision from God just weeks before. God told him there was going to be a young American couple cross his path. God told him to adopt us as his American missionaries in his church. When he saw our faces he could not keep from staring because we were the couple he saw in the vision. He was one of the judges on the Supreme Court in Panama. From that time on, all of our legal papers were done free by him!

Needless to say, we became
very good friends. He pastored
a large Spanish church in the
outskirts of Panama City. I
believe he had 1,500 members, but
if everyone came at the same time
there would be 2,300 people in the
church. The church was an air

tent. It looked like a large caterpillar. The church was wild and crazy for God! We instantly bonded with the people. Little did we know that they would play such a large role in the next season of our lives.

This was the end of the first chapter of our lives.

mind that they had something to do with the next season of our life.

Dennis began going down to the jungle on a regular basis with the pastor. Soon the pastor quit going and Dennis and another missionary friend of ours named Kevin Singer began going for two-week stretches. I was home-schooling the kids so it was impossible for us to go.

I will never forget the first time we all went with Dennis to the Darien Jungle. We owned a little four-seat Toyota work jeep. It was perfect for the rough terrain. The jeep was too small for our family. Our oldest son was 13 years old, but he was six feet tall. The back seats were bench seats that faced each other. They were meant for one person on each bench. Needless to say, they were not very large.

We were driving for about a half hour when Dennis said, "Oh, I forgot to tell you that I invited a friend to go with us today." We stopped at the man's house and out came this man that weighed about 200 pounds. I knew he was getting my seat. I just kind of glared at Dennis as if to say, "We will talk about this little surprise later."

Dennis is not a person who thinks of many details. The journey was 10 hours on roads that were not even suited for cattle. There were several places where the holes were deep enough that semi-trucks were stuck in them. All you could see was the top of the truck. The hole had totally swallowed it. The farther we went, the more isolated it became. Trees overlapped the road and you could hardly see the sunlight. There were people here and there, but it seemed to be basically unpopulated. This picture shows the local bus stop.

About seven hours into our trip the kids began getting hungry and thirsty, so I asked

Dennis if maybe we could stop to eat. He said, "Eat?" I said, "Yeah, the kids are hungry." "Oh," he said, "I forgot to tell you there are no restaurants in the jungle."

We continued another four hours and the kids began to get really restless. They wanted to get out and stretch their legs. The jeep had no air conditioning in it and the back windows did not open. The road was so dusty and Dennis was driving so fast that our hair was all white with dust.

We stopped for about half an hour. He took the kids down to a little creek and they all swam and got wet with no clothes to change into. The man went up to one of the grass huts and asked for some fruit for the kids. They gave us bananas and oranges, I believe. The kids were content after that. So we climbed back into the jeep and continued traveling for three more hours. It was about 2 p.m. by that time.

We turned off of the main road and headed down a path that I was convinced was not a road. It went up a mountain and down into a valley. The path was very dangerous and you could easily fall off the side of the road at any given time. The bridges were two trees thrown across the riverbed. They were very slippery and some even had a hole halfway across the crossing.

After about one hour of driving in even rougher terrain, we finally arrived in a very primitive Indian village. Their housing consisted of a wooden floor about eight feet off the ground. It had a grass roof, but no walls. They entered into the housing by shimmying up a pole that had wedges cut out for their feet to grab a hold of. The children up to about age 10 were naked. The women wore very colorful tribal skirts. Each woman had handmade beaded necklaces draped around her neck. They did not wear any tops. The majority of the men wore loin cloths. They seemed to be friendly but I wasn't too sure about it. For sure no one seemed to be a Christian or had even heard of Jesus.

They had a darkness about their eyes that led you to believe that they could turn on you at any time. No one smiled at you. Everyone just stared like they had never seen a white person before.

We stopped at a riverbed that had canoes tied up to the port. Dennis said, "I have a big surprise for you!" I was thinking, "Oh, no, not another surprise!" The kids were thrilled as we got into a large canoe that must have been made for about 30 people. About 16 other people got into the canoe with us. They were all carrying plastic containers and old cans with the lids off. I thought it was kind of strange but did not say anything.

We left the port of Puerto Lara and went about two hours out into the ocean and down into a bay. The canoe had an outboard motor attached to it and oars tied onto the side of the canoe.

The area was very beautiful and interesting. We were in the thick of nature with a capital "N." Beautiful birds lined the bay, and monkeys were jumping from treetop to treetop. We got out of the canoe and went up to the capital city of Darien. The name of that city was La Palma. I thought to myself, "I am really in trouble if this is the capital city." There was one stony road, one restaurant, and a police station.

We ate at the restaurant very cautiously. I will never forget what they served us. It was fish head soup. The fish head was looking at you every bite that you took. I am not a picky eater and I was starving by that time. The kids thought it was the coolest thing they had ever eaten. Jason, our middle son, is very adventurous like Dennis. He poked the eyes of the fish out with his fork and ate them. Everyone was grossed out, but he thought they were really good. The kids were obviously on the trip of a lifetime. This was so much better than Disney World in their minds!

After we ate, everyone got back into the canoe. The Indians had a worried look on their faces. About a half an hour out into the bay I understood what their concern was. The man with us spoke their language. The Indians said we were hitting the bay at the wrong time of the day. Soon after that, large waves came crashing into the canoe.

They were four feet high on each side of the canoe. I don't think that I have ever been so scared in all of my life. The kids sat in shock and did not know what was going on. All of the water made them have to go to the bathroom and, of course, there were no toilets anywhere. A large wave crashed on top of us inside the canoe. This is when I found out what the plastic bottles and tin cans were for. Everybody began to bail out the water as fast as they could. An elderly Indian man looked at me and said something. I asked the translator what he was saying. "Many people die in these shark-infested waters." I was not thrilled about the information he was sharing with me! Dennis looked back at me with a large grin from ear to ear. He put his thumbs up like he was having the time of his life. I gritted my teeth and said, "Dennis, when we get back to dry land I am going to kill you!"

At that time I heard the Lord say to me in what seemed to be an audible voice, "What makes you think you are going to get back to dry land?" He then continued that when you harbor unforgiveness in your heart it is hard to pray for safety. My mind was hallucinating. I saw a large newspaper as big as the sky. The headlines read: MISSIONARY FAMILY ALL DIE AT SEA! I knew I had to forgive Dennis if we were ever going to get out of this alive. By this time the kids were crying and scared out of their wits.

Then, if that was not enough, the outboard motor stopped. They could not get it to start again. One Indian stood on top of what they called the lookout point of the canoe and began whistling. I heard another whistle and then another. The whistling went all the way down the bay. About three hours later another canoe came up beside of us. By then it was so dark that you couldn't even see your own hand. No one expected to be on the bay at night so no one had a flashlight. The canoe bumped up alongside of ours. The waves had calmed down but the Indians kept telling us to keep all hands inside the canoe. I asked the translator if they brought another outboard motor with them for our canoe. He said, "No, we need to get out of this canoe and into that one."

The water was very rough and choppy, and the canoes kept drifting apart. I am not a very coordinated person naturally. Of course, Dennis was the first one to jump from our canoe over into the other one. He was born coordinated. The new canoe had many lights on it. You could see Dennis's grin even in the dark. He began helping the kids into the canoe. One by one we all jumped from one canoe to the other one. It was about three hours back to the original little port of Puerto

Lara. It rained several times on us and we were cold and very wet. The breeze coming off of the ocean was very cold.

By this time I had made up my mind that this was the first and last trip that the kids and I would ever make to the jungle. The thought about killing Dennis entered my mind once again since we would soon be safely on land. When the canoe arrived they pulled up to the muddy shore and tied the canoe. We got out of the canoe and sank up to our knees in mud. It seemed like quicksand because it ate all of our shoes. The Indians just laughed and laughed. At this point I could not find humor in anything.

Standing on the bank of the riverbed was a small little boy with blonde hair. He looked to be about 2 years old. I thought it odd to see a child with blonde hair here. I later found out it was because the sun had bleached it out. His eyes penetrated down deep inside of me. My heart began to cry for that little boy for some reason. He was naked and his stomach was 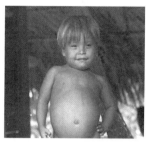 the size of a basketball. I could not get the look of his little eyes out of my heart. They seemed to torment me. I asked the Lord why he touched me so deeply. He said, "You are the only hope that he has. He will die if you refuse to move here with Dennis." I thought, "Oh, great, nothing like a little guilt to deal with on top of this horrible day!"

We got back into the jeep and started on our long trip home. Dennis just could not quit talking. He kept saying, "Don't you just love this, Jeanne?" I could not respond because of that little boy's eyes. The road now had turned into pure mud and we literally slid all the way down the mountain and onto the main road. The trip home seemed to last for an eternity. The kids fell asleep from pure exhaustion.

When we arrived back in the city it was very late. The jeep could not be seen for the mud that covered it. It was a quick reminder of what we had been through.

Dennis must have talked all night. I was extremely quiet because in the natural there was no way I could handle moving down there. There was no electricity, no running water, no toilets, and no houses to rent. There was just no way! But I could not get rid of the look in that little boy's eyes. I kept reasoning in my mind why we could not do this. I remembered the promise that I had made to God, but all that I could do was cry. I knew if I told Dennis that I could not handle living there that he would quit going and he would find something else to do in the Spanish church.

By now we were one of the associate pastors of the church and the pastor was training Dennis to be his right-hand man. The pastor went to the United States every year to speak in churches. He had already asked Dennis if he would pastor the church while he was in the States. Dennis had agreed to do that for him. The pastor was going to be gone for three months. The only problem with that plan was that Dennis's heart was definitely in the Darien Jungle. There was no doubt in my mind that he was called there to preach the gospel.

During those three months our missionary friend Kevin kept going to the jungle. He lived with us and when he would come back he and Dennis would stay up all night talking. I felt so bad because I was standing in the way of the call of God on Dennis's life. That was the very thing that I never wanted to do.

When Pastor Rory came back he approached Dennis about buying the land from the elderly gentleman in the church. He said we could pay it off little by little. He could see the call to the jungle on Dennis's life. Dennis asked me if it would bother me if he bought the land. I told him that it would be fine with me. So he began making payments on the land, and he continued making trips to the jungle with our missionary friend.

It was really hard on the family with Dennis gone two weeks out of each month. Kevin had decided to go back home on furlough, so Dennis was going alone to the jungle. Many nights the Lord would wake me up to pray for him. Finally I told the Lord that if I consented to move to the jungle He was going to have to give me a lot of grace. So I told Dennis that we wanted to move there to not be away from him so much. He was so excited that he could not quit kissing me. I had spoken the words out of my mouth and there was no way that I could take them back now. I had made the commitment!

LIFE IN THE DARIEN

We began going with him for two weeks at a time and then come back into the city for two weeks. I thought this would help us to adjust to the huge difference in cultures.

On our second trip down there we stayed in a little village called Los

Monos. Los Monos was a very warm and loving village. I later found out that Los Monos meant "the monkeys" in Spanish.

The people obviously had never seen a white girl, but for some reason they hovered around me to make me feel like I was one of them. I supernaturally could understand their language. At this time most of them did not speak Spanish. They taught me everything. I cried all of the time. They would say, "Don't cry, Jeanne. We will help you." I felt so helpless. I did not know how to do anything. I had always been very independent and self-sustaining. Now I had to rely on others for everything.

I found their culture to be interesting. I have always loved different cultures.

The women were so peaceful. Nothing upset them. They all wore tribal skirts and no tops and all kinds of handmade colorful beads. The men wore loin cloths. The little girls wore the tribal skirt also. The little boys dressed like their dads. On special occasions they painted their bodies with a natural dye that comes from the Jagua nut.

They taught me how to cook like they did, with what we call kindling wood. This special kind of wood is called leña there. They put three pieces of it together and set a large kettle where the wood met in the middle and then lit it.

There were no stores to buy food so we ate off of the land and

caught our own meat and fish. They were farmers and ate what they grew. The Indians shared everything with us.

Rice was a staple in their diet. They would harvest it and store it in 100-pound sacks. Then they would clean it as they used it. They would throw it up in the air and the wind blew

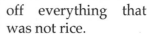

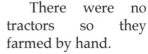

off everything that was not rice.

There were no tractors so they farmed by hand.

There was no drinking water except the river water, so the Indians caught their drinking water from the rains with a piece of tin that ran off of

their grass roofs. I was not too comfortable with that method since I knew rats and bats lived in the thatched roofs. They also carried their water from the river to the house. Some got it out of the river way up stream. The Indians washed their clothing in one area and used it for bathroom facilities down the river that flowed out to the bay which eventually washed out into the ocean. The river was used for everything in their lives. It was their lifeline.

I chose to get our drinking water from the river and put a little bleach in it to purify it. Then we prayed really hard over it!

The Indians taught me how to bathe in the river. That was a real issue for me because I had very thick hair that hung down to my waist. It was so hard to get the soap out of it. They took me up river where the current was and told me to lay against the current. Sure enough, it got all of the soap out of my hair. None of them used shampoo. They did not even know what it was. They used some kind of soap that they made. It was full of lye. They used it for everything. They did the

dishes, washed their cloths, and also bathed with it.

I did not know how to wash clothing in the river. Having four kids you can imagine how many clothes I had to wash. For some reason our children were always dirty and full of mud. Their clothes were very dirty. It did not take us long before we let our boys run in play shorts and Jennifer in little short outfits. Blue jeans were too hot and definitely too hard to wash. It took days  for them to dry even though the sun was very hot and sometimes it would be over 100 degrees.

The Indians gave me a bar of soap and a rock. They showed me how to use my hands as a scrub board and to run the clothes across the rock. Then they would rinse out the soap in the river and slap the clothing very hard against the large rock we were standing on. It was hard but it really got your clothing clean.

My hands bled every time I washed clothes because of how hard the lye was on my skin.

Of course, my skin was very delicate and not toughened up to the elements yet like theirs. Their skin was like leather and basically nothing bothered them. The bottoms of their feet were as tough as a leather sole on a shoe. They could walk on rocks and never even feel it.

After we moved into the tents, I washed clothes in the river for a couple of years. Then a good friend of ours shipped me a wringer washing machine. It was so nice because it really got the water out of the clothes. The clothes were a lot cleaner and dried quicker.

I now have an electric washer which I want to kiss every time I use it! I have never owned a dryer because the clothes dry so quick when the temperature is always high, 90-120 degrees.

LIVING WITH THE INDIANS

The Indians worked in the field every day and bathed with the lye soap every day. They were very clean people! I would share my shampoo and conditioner with them. They really loved it and soon the word "shampoo" was known all over the village. Every time I would bathe, all the kids would come to get some shampoo. Everyone had a head of shampoo in the river. They laughed and laughed as they would blow the shampoo suds in each other's face. It was such a happy time for them.

Our children quickly adapted to living with the Indians. There were no schools anywhere in the jungle at this time. The kids all had chores to do, but every evening they ran to the river and swam and then played soccer and then swam again. They did not have a care in this world.

The Indians taught our children everything. One of the first things that they learned to do was fish. Their idea of fishing was not exactly what our kids were used to. They all wore a water mask and had a spear with a very sharp edge. They laid on the bottom of the riverbed until the fish they wanted passed by. Then they would stab it and throw it up on the riverbank into a 5-gallon bucket. The fish were plentiful so there was always enough to go around.

They taught the kids how to walk in the jungle and keep from getting bitten by one of the 48 different types of deadly poisonous snakes. The Indians walked barefooted but I made our kids wear their flip-flops.

Our children thought they were in seventh heaven. They had been introduced to a whole new world, a world free from life's pressures. There was no peer pressure in the villages. None of the children were ever disrespectful to their parents. They believed the oldest man in the village was the wisest man because he had lived longer than anyone.

Our family's welfare was definitely a project that included the whole village. Their love for us overwhelmed me.

The Indians' attitude in life was so wonderful. It touched my life in a deep way. They were very happy people and they laughed about everything. Even in tragedy they would find something to laugh about. In hard times they would count the heads and say, "Well, nobody died!" This was a common saying when there would be a tragedy.

I remember one time there was a tropical storm. It was awful! The rivers rose 16 feet in just one day. The Indians laughed and said, "We will all have to sleep on the rooftops tonight!" When the water rose over the rooftops they merely got everyone in the canoes and rode to higher ground. That night the people were counting heads to make sure everyone was there, and every head was accounted for. All their homes were destroyed (90 families lost their homes in that tropical storm). They sat around a campfire that night and laughed and laughed about how they all had to keep going to higher ground. Then they said, "Tomorrow we will have to go down river to get the wood from our houses and rebuild." They were convinced all their houses were relocated in the next village down! To them, the only important thing in life was their family. Everything else could be replaced. They taught us to laugh in the middle of a tragedy or hard time.

If they do have a death, the way they look at death is beautiful. The parents tell everyone that the richest man in the universe adopted their child and that no one should be sad because the child had everything he ever wanted in life.

If an adult died, they would set a coffee pot on a small campfire near the house. When people die the family washes the body with alcohol then dresses them. The family makes the casket and places the body in the casket. They have the viewing and the funeral the same day. The family digs the hole to bury the casket. The body is buried within 24 hours. People do not bring food or anything like Americans do.

In the area of crime, the greatest disgrace was to be found stealing something that did not belong to you. Their punishment had a lasting affect on our children. The person was put in wooden stocks in front of the whole village and he stayed there for three days and

nights. Both hands and their neck was locked in the wooden stocks and the person was positioned on his knees. Needless to say there was not much crime in the village.

You never heard of a baby being conceived out of wedlock. If this happened they made the girl live in the jungle away from the rest of the village. She was shunned by the village. She would have her child all alone. For the sake of the child they would accept her and the baby back in the village after the baby was born.

They did not marry like we were accustomed to. The father of the girl would choose a young man who was around 18 years old for his daughter. He would study the young man and make sure they were compatible. The girls were given in marriage at 14 years old. The girl would be put into the hammock of the young man. Once their covenant was sealed they would go to live with the girl's parents. They lived with her parents for five years. During those five years the parents taught them how to live together as man and wife.

When the babies were born, the girl's mother was always the midwife for the birth of her grandchildren. They made a tent out of a white sheet in the house, and the girl and her mother stayed in that tent until the baby was born. As soon as the baby was born they would take the liquid out of the baby's mouth and nose and then hand the child to the father who would walk around with the child and tell the child all about his Indian heritage. The Indians highly value every child that's born. The sign of God's blessings on your life is how many children He has blessed you with. They are very loving with their children and respect them. They are never laughed at or made fun of. No harsh words are ever spoken to them.

At the age of 4 the young boys follow their dads into the jungle to work. They are taught from very young how to handle a machete.

The little girls at that age were responsible for washing their own underwear and towel. They learned to wash and do all of the household chores.

At the age of 6 the children were given the

responsibility to watch a newborn baby. It was a real honor to be able to watch your brothers and sisters. They did not think that it was an inconvenience or something they did not want to do. They all loved watching each other and would carefully take care of each other.

The children were not selfish at all. If someone would give them a bottle of soda they would make sure that everyone in the family had a sip from it before they took a second drink.

They did not make fun of each other or speak harsh words. They teased each other, but no one ever got mad. It was all in fun and everyone knew it was. You almost never saw the children fight or argue.

After the young man and his new bride lived with her parents for five years, everyone would pitch in and build them a house of their own. The house was so close to her parents that they could throw a board across the floor and go visit each other. Everyone lived close to their families.

The Indians live on reservations of land. No one owns their own land. The chief of the village gives every family a piece of land to farm according to the size of their family.

Each village has a cacique, which is like a mayor and a chief. The whole village votes on everything going on in the village and decides what is good for the community.

The Panamanian police have no jurisdiction on the Indian reservation. The chief is the final authority and he passes sentence for the crimes committed. One very interesting thing is that the whole village comes together to hear the case presented. The whole village votes whether the person is guilty or not. Their ways of dealing with things are totally different than ours. At that time there were not many crimes

committed. Today it is a different story.

It was the Indian culture that if you were not Indian born you had to earn the right to speak, so we were not allowed to share from our hearts for a period of two years. We were there to learn how to live in the jungle. We could not give our opinion about anything. No one asked our opinion anyway until we had passed the approval test. They wanted to make sure that they knew our hearts were pure towards them before they trusted us.

We lived with the Indians in Los Monos for two years. After that time the chief said that he felt that we knew enough to survive on our own. The bonds we made during those two years are still very deep today, more than 30 years later. At times they will tease me about different things that I did not know how to do. It is funny now, but it was not then!

This ended the second chapter of our lives and prepared us for the next. Each season in your life prepares you for the next season. If you try to learn all that you can in each season then your next season will help you advance to a deeper level in God. The next season is always a step into abundance. It never goes backwards but is always advancing in blessings.

CHAPTER THREE
MOVING INTO TENTS
ON OUR OWN LAND

At this time we told all of our friends in Panama City goodbye and prepared to move to the jungle on our own land. Our two-week adjustments had come to an end. We were now going to move to the jungle and live there full time.

REALITY

Dennis decided to take me on a preview run before we actually moved. I was totally unprepared for what I encountered. I had never seen the land before that he had purchased. We got out of the jeep and the weeds were way over our heads. Dennis saw the look on my face and said, "Don't worry, Jeanne. I will make us a path." He then proceeded to get his machete out of its case and began cutting like a wild man. He used the machete like he was born swinging one!

We got into the land about a mile and I panicked. It was like reality hit me that we were going to live in this dense jungle that I was walking in. Dennis turned around and said, "Jump on my back and I will piggyback you the rest of the way." That did not work so well so he carried me to the place where he wanted to build our house. The view was beautiful if you could get over the density of it all.

Dennis was hysterically happy. However, walking in the next season of my life was going to require me to face some of my greatest fears.

I was really afraid of snakes. When I read up on the Darien Jungle I learned that there were 48 different kinds of deadly poisonous snakes in the jungle. The smallest ones were more deadly than the others because they had never released any of their venom. It was pure. One snake can give birth to up to 50 snakes at

one time. Right then I wished that I did not have that knowledge! One of the most deadliest snakes is the Bushmaster who is very aggressive and hides in bushes. It would literally chase you and bite you not once, but several times. This land had never been lived on before so it was full of bushes. I just knew Bushmasters lived under every bush and were waiting for me to pass by.

There were seven Quipo trees, each standing at least 150 feet tall. They were just about the most awesome thing that I had ever seen in all of my life. Quipo trees are about six feet in diameter. The bark of the tree is slick and smooth like the hide of an elephant. There are no branches on the tree until the top of the tree. At the top it spreads its branches all over the sky. I used to pretend it was God's umbrella of protection over us. Dennis said that he wanted to build our house there so that every time we got overwhelmed we could look up at those trees and remember how big our God is. Those trees proved to be a great inspiration to me over the years. In the summer, orchids covered the tops of the trees, making a beautiful sea of fresh-smelling flowers.

All the way home my mind was thinking about what we needed to take to live there. There was no electricity and no running water. I packed a box full of tin plates, one around, and cups. I brought two big iron pots to cook on an open fire. I stuck my best friend after God and Dennis...my coffee pot...in the box. I kept that pot for many years to remind me of the very special talks that I had with God over my morning coffee. I also packed a pillow and a sleeping bag for each of us and some towels. Along with our clothing, that was all that we took to move.

The next day Dennis had been saying goodbye to all of his friends in Panama City and he came home really excited. Dennis had hundreds of friends everywhere. There was almost no one he did not know. He had a chaplain friend named Rev. Harvey Brown who told him that every so many years the American government throws away their tents. Dennis received one of the tents and was sure it was a gift from God!

We moved out of our duplex and put all our furniture that was given to us in a small one-bedroom apartment. This way when we came into town once a month to buy supplies we would have a place to live. Hotels were expensive and eating out three meals a day for six people was just out of the question. At this time the boys were 15, 13 and 11 years old. Chris alone could eat five sandwiches for lunch. Those boys could put away some serious amounts of food. Jennifer ate like a bird. The boys took after their dad because Dennis could out eat them all!

THE BIG MOVE

That weekend we made the big move. Dennis stopped first in the village of Los Monos and got workers to come and clear off a place to put up the tent. They cleared off about two acres of our land. We owned 68 acres of very dense jungle. Dennis was so excited that he could hardly wait to get the tent up. He barely made it to nightfall. He wanted to carry me over the threshold, but the zipper door did not permit anyone to walk upright into the tent.

That night we all laid there and no one made a sound. The tent did not need windows because there were so many holes in it that you could count the stars in the sky. Thankfully there were no holes on the zippered floor. The tent measured about 12 feet x 14 feet in size. Dennis slept like a baby that night. He was so happy. The kids thought it was the thrill of a lifetime. I laid there crying and talking to God. I told Him that I loved Him so much that I was going to keep my word, but

that this was so much bigger than I. I could feel Him smiling and saying, "You are going to make it just fine, Jeanne." We slept in that tent for 2 ½ years, but we lived in a ranchito, which is a small thatched-roof house with no floor and no walls.

The next day I woke up before the sun rose. Dennis had bought me a Coleman camping stove to cook on. I put on my very first pot of coffee on our new land. I made it extra strong that morning!

I asked Dennis where I could get some water to cook and clean

dishes, etc. We had brought some drinking water with us. He quickly took me down a dense path to a little creek. It was a very nice little creek. I had the feeling that I would be spending a lot of time there in the future.

That little creek became the place where I did all of our laundry. It also became my crying place. When things got too hard, I always made a trip to the creek to get some water. The water had to be carried in 5-gallon buckets. The bucket weighed 40 pounds when full of water. It was normally one of the chores for the kids to carry the water for the day up to the campsight.

I tried really hard not to cry in front of Dennis or the children. Before I moved to the jungle I was not a person who cried much. But then, I was in control of my life. If the kids thought it was hard on me, then everything would turn into a major attitude of it being too hard on them. Dennis would get really discouraged if he saw me crying.

God and I began to build a very strong relationship. I talked to Him all day long and most of the night. He knew my greatest fears and always knew what to say to me when I was overwhelmed. There is an old Chinese proverb that says, "You can adjust to anything with just an attitude adjustment." I asked the Lord to help me change my attitude. He really came through with flying colors. He told me that His grace was sufficient for me, but I must choose to walk in it. Every morning I would say out loud over the coffee pot, "I choose to walk in the grace of God for the call of God on our lives." It helped so much! Every time things would get challenging I would say out loud, "God's grace is sufficient for me." I began thinking that this was not such a bad place after all. I rather enjoyed how peaceful it was.

I have always loved nature. In the mornings the birds would wake us up singing. Monkeys were swinging from tree to tree and always putting on a show. The butterflies were abundant and in every color imaginable. My favorite one was the very large royal blue butterfly. The skies at night were covered with millions of very bright stars. You could watch them forever. It was common to see a falling star. I could always pick out the North Star from all of the other stars. There was no pollution anywhere so the sky was clear and bright.

GOD AND STARS

I taught the kids the Bible through the stars and the planets. We would talk for hours while watching the beauty of God's creative hands. He is truly a magnificent God. Who could compare to His infinite wisdom? I stand in awe of how detailed He created everything. The solar system is just too marvelous for words. You can learn a lot from studying the stars.

> *Those who are wise shall shine like the brightness of the firmament, and those who turn many to righteousness like the stars forever.*

> **DANIEL 12:3 (NKJV)**

> *"Then the righteous will shine forth as the sun in the kingdom of their Father. He who has ears to hear, let him hear!"*

> **MATTHEW 13:43 (NKJV)**

A friend of mine shared a teaching with me that explained exactly what I was feeling at that time...

Some ministers are like the great, guiding North Star, and others are like brief shooting stars.

The North Star has remained in place since man has been on the earth. Its brilliance is permanent and its light has been available for every generation. The North Star is dependable. Sometimes it is called the pole star. It appears stationary while other stars seem to revolve around it.

During a voyage, and definitely after a storm, mariners knew they could depend upon the North Star to reset their compasses. The North Star is always where it is supposed to be - in the north. It's not because it's the brightest, but it is the most dependable. Millions have been directed and saved by this star.

On the other hand, a shooting star occurs when a chunk of metallic or stony matter enters earth's atmosphere from outer space. Air friction heats the chunk so that it glows and creates a trail of gases and melted particles. Most of these stars disintegrate under the friction and glow for about a second.

Stars are literally born. In science they have discovered that there are clouds of gas in space that are star makers. A mixture of gas and dust under pressure begins to heat and when a certain core temperature is reached a wind is formed in the core that births a star from out of the cloud of gas into space.

The core of a star is composed only of gas. The core temperature must be kept constant - a very high degree of heat. The outer layers are composed of compressed dust.

To shine, a star radiates energy into space. This energy is a result of parts of hydrogen gas in the core bumping against each other resulting in the likeness of nuclear burning.

A star can expand out of control or collapse on itself if the forces of gravity and internal gas pressure are not balanced at each point of the star.

If burning stops, pressure in the core drops and the star begins to cool. At this point the star collapses on itself. Sometimes in a collapse the core will reheat and restart energy. The star will settle into a new stable phase - but it will be a shorter time until the next collapse.

A cycle of cooling, collapsing, and restarting may continue until the star's core becomes iron. At this point no energy can be generated in the iron core. The energy can only be generated in the hydrogen gas. The outer layers of the star crash into the core resulting in a massive explosion.

We are born into this earth as dust. Just as the earth lay without form and void, so are we. Before we are born again and become a new creation, the Spirit of God hovers over us. When God sent Jesus - the Word, the life, the light that lights every man that comes into the world - those two parts, the Spirit and the Word, began bumping together and a spiritual nuclear explosion of energy happened on the inside of us. The life and the light of God exploded forth inside us! The wind of the Spirit blew us into this universe as stars of God.

What causes us to burn as dependable and stable as the North Star? The burning of the Spirit and the Word in the core of our spirit causes us to shine forth.

The entrance of Your words gives light;....

PSALM 119:130 (NKJV)

The words that I speak to you are spirit, and {they} are life.

JOHN 6:63 (NKJV)

Even when the forces of the world come against us and batter our outer layers, the consistency of the Word and Spirit in our lives keeps the forces from the outside in balance.

> *You are of God, little children, and have overcome them, because He who is in you is greater than he who is in the world.*

1 JOHN 4:4 (NKJV)

Greater is the pressure on the inside than the pressure on the outside. When the burning and explosion of the Spirit and the Word slow on the inside of me, it allows the pressure to drop in my core. Cooling begins which allows the outside pressure to collapse on my core. Sometimes that restarts and once again stabilizes, but it takes a toll on my soul.

If we remain in the cycle of cooling, collapsing, and restarting, it causes our heart to harden. When our heart hardens there is nothing to generate energy to shine. The outer layers crash into the core, resulting in an explosion that demolishes the star.

> *Cast not away therefore your confidence, which hath great recompense of reward. For ye have need of patience, that, after ye have done the will of God, ye might receive the promise.*

HEBREWS 10:35-36

Patience, endurance, constancy, consistency. In other words, no matter what the pressure on the outside, I keep the resources of the Word and Spirit fired up in my core to shine brighter and brighter.

> *Knowing this, that the trying of your faith worketh patience. But let patience have her perfect work, that ye may be perfect and entire, wanting nothing.*

JAMES 1:3-4

Pressure from the outside should cause the pressure on the inside to grow brighter and brighter. You see, without outer pressure we would expand out of control.

Shooting stars are caused by thinking on the wrong things, getting off the Word of God, off of the vision God gives you, focusing on self and self-promotion, and seeking notoriety and publicity in ministry. We lose our effectiveness in the kingdom and in the ministry.

I felt the Lord ask me what legacy I was going to leave. Am I going to be a North Star or a shooting star? I was determined to remain a North Star and not lose my inward flame for God. Being a North Star took a decision, a decision that meant no matter how rough things got, going home was no option.

OUR NEW LIFE

I have never seen Dennis so happy! It made me willing to stick this out because there is nothing more rewarding to a woman than to see her husband glowing with happiness. He had found what he had been looking for over such a long time. Everything to him was a big adventure. Nothing was hard or impossible to achieve.

Dennis had an answer for every challenge. He has always been very quick to come up with solutions to impossible situations. I asked him what we were going to do for a toilet. He smiled real big and said, "I have already thought about that. Close your eyes." So I closed my eyes and was almost afraid to open them again. He went somewhere close by and then he said, "Okay, you can open your eyes now." When I opened my eyes I saw that he had a chrome chair with the cushion out of the middle of it. He said, "Ta-da! This is our toilet. You just move it around when you are done." I stood there stunned with no words to respond. Unfortunately, he was serious! The temperature got to be 120 degrees during the day, and I got to feeling like a branded cow after awhile, but it served its purpose for many years!

When we adjusted to the jungle I knew that we had to establish a schedule. I had to get the kids back into the routine of having school each day, so I began to home-school them.

Dennis decided that he would farm part of the land so we could live off the land. He went to the village of Los Monos and hired some workers. They came to work that next week. When the Indians worked on the farm they would spend their lunch hour with Dennis.

PREACHING THE GOSPEL

This is the time that Dennis began preaching the gospel. I would cry in the tent because he had become everything that I had asked God for. He preached with such conviction and integrity. I was bursting with pride. He had earned the right to speak into the lives of the Indians because they knew his heart.

They were full of questions. They first asked him why he had moved there with his family. One of the Indians was an elderly man named Rudy Barcoriso who said he was 76 years old at that time. Until this day when you ask Rudy he will tell you he is 76 years old. Dennis was only 38 years old then, but Rudy could work circles around Dennis. As Dennis began to share, Rudy just smiled. He said, "You are an answer to our prayers, Dennis. For years we heard there was a God but no one would explain who He was or how to live for Him. We heard about Him but did not know Him. God has sent you to us to reveal Himself to our people."

Every lunch hour Dennis would share a passage of the Bible. The Indians lingered on each word that fell from Dennis's lips. Dennis had been silent for two years and now he had earned the right to speak into their lives. They loved him and trusted him with their lives. We were not Indian born, but we had become part of their lives and their family.

Rudy asked Dennis to come and hold a large meeting in the middle of his village so everyone could hear about Dennis's God. In their custom everything had to be cleared by the chief. Dennis asked the chief for permission to have an open-air meeting. He just smiled at Dennis and said, "Of course you can." This was the favor of God because the chief was the witch doctor!

The next night Dennis set up a meeting in the place where we had lived for two years. He was going to use a loud speaker. Before the meeting the chief asked if he could use the sound system to talk to his people. Dennis felt a little insecure about it, but he consented. The chief got up and told his people to listen to everything that Dennis said because he was a good man.

This was the night that the gifts of miracles began to establish our ministry in the Darien Jungle.

Dennis preached his heart out on "God Our Savior." I sat there crying because I was so proud of him. He was such a godly man and

FOOTSTEPS OF FAITH

I had grown to deeply love and respect the call of God on his life. I was so glad that I chose to face my greatest fear because I had found the greatest riches in life. There is absolutely nothing so rewarding as walking in God's call on your life.

There were some women in a nearby hut that kept making so much noise that Dennis could hardly be heard. Dennis asked Alberto, one of the teens, to go over there and ask the people not to make so much noise. When Alberto got there the noise became louder and louder. The voices, chanting to the devil, began screaming in terror. About that time a wind blew across Dennis's shoulder with so much strength that we thought a tropical storm was about to hit...but it was not the season for tropical storms.

Soon Alberto came back with three women following him. They were totally blind. He asked them what had happened. They said that they were trying to destroy the crusade by chanting to the devil when a wind blew in and knocked them all to the ground. When they got up, they were totally blind. Then they said a voice came to them and said, "Never mock the one true God or a man preaching about Him." The fear of God fell on the village. They had witnessed the power of God to defend Himself.

Dennis laid hands on the women and they were instantly healed and their sight returned to them. The compassion of God was so strong that everyone was crying. The Indians are not normally emotional people. I have lived here since 1981 and I can count on one hand how many times that I have seen one of them cry. Without a doubt they saw the judgment of God fall on people making fun of Him. Why would He strike them blind and then turn around and heal them? These women were witches and working against Him. You knew that you were definitely on "miracle" ground. When Dennis made an altar call they were the first in line to get born again. Almost the whole village got born again that night. Then he called for the sick to come forward. There must have been close to four hundred people there that evening.

Through the crowd pushed a woman that I had never met before. She had walked from another village carrying a little boy. You could feel the fever coming from her son's body. When she got up to where the people were being prayed for I saw why the fever was so high. The child was about 12 months old. He had a tumor the size of a grapefruit in his groin area. Dennis prayed for the little boy. He felt the power of God go into the child's body. The tumor did not disappear immediately. Dennis told the woman that the manifestation would come and not to

58

give up hope.

Many people were healed that night as God moved mightily through their lives. There were a lot of sicknesses in the villages. Many people brought their children to be prayed for. Around 60% of the children did not reach their first birthday because of the many diseases in the jungle.

I remember one child who was almost dead when I took him into my arms. His little body was limp. He did not seem to have much life left in him. I held him up to my heart and began praying for him. The compassion of God came up from inside of me and I felt my whole body was on fire with the love of God. That baby's body began to jerk. He was instantly healed and wanted to nurse. That was the first time that I had ever felt the love and compassion of God move through my body. It changed my life. From that point on I had such a cry in my heart for the salvation and healing of these people.

The next night we continued the crusade. The woman who had the little boy with a tumor came running up to Dennis crying, "Look, Brother Cook, the tumor is gone!" She then gave her testimony in front of everyone in the crusade. She was the wife of one of the witch doctors in a nearby village. Ever since the boy was born he was sick and had the tumor. It kept getting larger and larger. She said her husband called upon all the power of the devil that he knew, but the boy kept getting worse. The night before, she was sitting in a nearby hut when the three witches were struck blind. She saw God restore their sight. She told her husband (the witch doctor) that she was taking the little boy over to be prayed for. Her husband followed her, arguing the whole way. She said when the boy was no better she kept saying, "The manifestation will come." How she knew to do that I do not know. To my knowledge no one had ever taught her to do that. The next morning the boy woke up totally healed. The woman accepted Jesus into her heart that night.

The crusade went on for one week. Miracles and signs and wonders were so present that it was a sign to the unbelievers that we served a powerful God. The witch doctors trembled and would not come near us. They said their powers were no match for the power that lived on the inside of us!

That was our first crusade and, with the manifestation of God's power, Dennis began preaching everywhere.

FOOTSTEPS OF FAITH

WITCH DOCTORS

The Darien Jungle is said to be one of the most powerful witchcraft strongholds. I have seen witch doctors turn into crows and fly away. I have seen witch doctors come walking over the water. They all travel in the supernatural realm. No one who works for the devil takes natural transportation. I have seen a horse talk with a message from the devil. I once saw a man riding a piece of cloth that looked like a magic carpet. When he got to dry land he got off the carpet, shook it out and used it as a towel to bathe with. He proclaimed a curse on the village if they accepted the gospel of the white man. He took the towel and shook it out again, got on it, and flew off over the water.

THE FIRST CHRISTIANS

Dennis began a Bible school to ground the new believers in the Word of God. Soon after that we started our first church.

It was a simple grass hut but everyone in the village came to the services. The presence of God was so strong during the meetings that people would be instantly healed just listening to the Word being preached. If you came in sick, you left healed.

Later we built a wood church. This was some ordeal, as we had to log our own trees and cut them into boards with a chainsaw. Then, deeper in the jungle, all the materials had to be taken in by canoe.

I began a children's

ministry at that time. No one had ever heard of a special class to establish children in the Word of God. Presently this is our fourth generation of Christians.

We give a curriculum and all of the supplies for one year to all of the new churches in Darien. When we ministered a lot in the city we gave the same blessings to many of the churches there. It is impossible to know how many children have been taught our curriculum over the years.

We also have a lot of crusades for children. We would like to thank Mrs. Jackie Long for all the years she has come here having special crusades. She has greatly impacted the Darien Jungle.

We would also like to recognize Miss Carolina Marriott who has been so faithful over all of the years that we have spent in Darien. She has been a translator and a good friend. Good friends in the ministry are priceless.

So many groups and faithful people have come here to help us. It is a blessing to see the Body of Christ all sharing their talents to complete the vision of the Lord.

The Bible school was very intense. Dennis taught four hours a day for three days a week. I remember one of his classes was on the names of Jesus. I went to the class when it was time for the final exams to make sure they had understood the teachings.

FOOTSTEPS OF FAITH

I quizzed them on different things. When I asked them what they thought of the class on the names of Jesus, their answers made my heart break with love for God for sending us to these people. What a blessing they have been to my life!

One of the students said, "In our culture we do not name our children until they are 6 months old. We want to study their character and their personality. Then we name the child after what we see in him or her. If Jesus's Father saw all those characteristics in His Son, then the Son is worthy to be honored."

They explained from their point of view...

If His name meant healer, then He must be able to heal.

If His name meant counselor, then He must counsel His people.

If His name meant omnipresent, then He must have the ability to be everywhere at all times.

If His name meant the slain Lamb of God, that means He gave His life for His Father. This type of love is very honorable and admirable.

If His name meant the giver of life, then He must be able to give life.

If His name meant provider, then He must provide for His children.

If His name meant love, then His love must be unconditional.

If His name meant King of Kings, then He must hold the title that is above all other kings.

If His name meant Prince of Peace, that means that He can give us peace of mind.

If His name meant mediator, that means He is always on our side.

They went on for about a half an hour sharing all of the names of the Lord and what it meant to them. I knew beyond a shadow of a doubt that these people had learned something very deep about God.

In their tradition they did not have any written contracts. A man's word was given and they shook hands and that was their contract. They believed that a man's worth was based on the value of his word.

When I asked them about their thoughts about the Bible being the Word of God, they quickly responded, "God the Father wrote His Word down for us. That means we can count on His Word being the truth and that it will never fail us." When something is written down it can never change in their culture. It is forever true.

They had no doubt that God the Father was a man of His word. He had established His power in so many ways to them in miracles and signs and wonders. They saw firsthand that this God held the supreme power in the entire world. No witch doctor or any other demon-possessed person could match this explosive power. They believed like little children and their lives were full of testimonies of God confirming His Word in their lives.

Needless to say I was proud to report to Dennis that they all learned what was taught better than he could ever imagine. It was not just a class to them. It was revelation knowledge that would change their lives forever.

They were the first generation of Christians in the Darien Jungle!

Dennis pastored that church for two years. After two years of training them in the Word of God in Bible school, Dennis appointed Elipio Opua as the first pastor of the village church. This young man spoke Spanish and the Indian dialects fluently. He was Dennis's translator. Dennis preached and taught in Spanish while Elipio would wait until Dennis was through and then preach the message in the Indian dialect. Sometimes Dennis would teach for three hours. Elipio had a photographic memory, so he memorized the Bible as Dennis preached it and then preached it in the Indian dialect. He never missed one scripture that Dennis used. At that time the Bible had not been translated in the Indian dialect. Their language had not been written down. Wycliffe Bible translators were working on it but had only completed the first three books of the epistles.

The people told us that they would watch our lives so that they would know what it means to be a follower of God. I guess it was biblical because Paul said to the believers in Corinth that they were their epistles written in their hearts that were known and read by all men (2 Corinthians 3:2).

Our walk with the Lord all of a sudden held such a responsibility to lead these innocent people in the right ways of the Bible. We began being careful about everything that we said and did, knowing they were watching. So much counted on our representation of God. There is a saying: "The world doesn't have a problem with Jesus Christ. They have a problem with our representation of Him."

The church grew daily and everyone in that village was eventually born again. Over the years this church has grown so large that we built a cement block church that was three times larger. We have seen so many miracles in that church over the years. That pastor resigned to go into the leadership of the carmaca. He is now one of the leading men who rule over all of the villages.

Dennis then appointed Luis Barcoriso as the new pastor. He is still the pastor today.

MARVELOUS MIRACLES

I want to share some of the marvelous things that we have seen in that church.

One little boy was born deaf and his grandfather would hold him in his arms and tell him the history of his ancestors and that he was born to be in line to be the chief of the village. Every night he went over and over about why he was born and what God's plan was for his life. When he was around 3 years old, the boy interrupted his grandfather and began asking questions. The compassion of God in the grandfather's heart reached out and healed that child's deafness. That little boy was totally healed and hears perfectly today over 20 years later!

There was a young boy who fell out of a coconut tree. He went to grab a coconut and lost his footing. He fell about 40 feet on his back. When his father saw his son falling, he screamed with all of the strength inside of him, "Jesus, my baby is falling." I was there when it happened and when he yelled the name of Jesus it was like the little 9-year-old boy fell like a feather and was gently placed on the ground. There was no thump or loud sound. The boy was totally conscience and in his right mind. We took him to the clinic to have him checked out and the doctor confirmed that we had seen a miracle. The boy was not even bruised!

Then there was a baby that died in the night. When he did not wake his mom up to feed him she turned over and noticed the little boy was not breathing. She took him into her arms and began to pray in other tongues. The child was raised from the dead and color came back into his body. No one knew how long the child had been dead, but one thing we knew for sure...he was alive and is still alive today!

Another time there was a little boy born to the chief of the village. His name was Elias Opua. When I saw him, I knew something was not right. We prayed for him and took him to the clinic to be checked out. The doctor confirmed the child was not normal. He said he was too small and that his hip bone was not connected to his leg. He said the child would be nothing more than a vegetable. The mother  spoke up and nearly screamed at the doctor. She said, "No! We serve a mighty God and He will heal my child." Every day she spoke the Word over this little boy.

At 18 months he still had not set up on his own. But when the baby turned 2, the mother sent word to me to come quickly. I came and she asked me to take her to the clinic. When we got there she called out the doctor by name and said, "I told you that God would heal my baby." The little boy ran across the floor into his mother's arms totally healed. Today he plays soccer and is an extremely bright child. He has been raised in Sunday school and loves God with his whole heart.

One of the students of the Bible school took her first-born child to visit her mother who lived three days away by canoe. When she got into the canoe there were 16 other people in the canoe. No one was a Christian but her. She knew everyone. A great storm came up in the ocean and the waves capsized the canoe. Everyone was bailing the water out in order to keep the canoe from sinking. When they were safe she looked down and her baby had washed out into the ocean. She stood up on the side of the canoe and said a quick prayer, "God, help me find my baby."

She dove down into the blackness of the ocean and her lungs were about to burst because she did not have any more air in them. She said, "Jesus, help me!" With one more grab into the darkness she grabbed the hand of her little baby. She did not think that she had enough air in her lungs to make it to the top of the water. She cried out in her heart once again and asked Jesus to help her. She said it was like a giant hand pushed her to the top of the ocean. There was so much force in the push that she was there before she even completed her prayer. When she made it to the top, she put the child gently inside the boat. The people's eyes were full of compassion. The baby was dead. He had drowned in the deep waters of the ocean in that violent storm. The young girl saw the look in everyone's eyes and she picked up her child's lifeless body and began speaking and groaning in other tongues. She prayed with all of her heart for over three hours and her prayers were interrupted by the sweet sound of her baby coughing up water. The child had been dead for more than three hours. He was totally perfect with no retardation! Today he is studying to be a forest ranger. He is a mighty man of God and plays the keyboard in the church.

One day we were asked to pray for a little girl who was 4 years old. She had what they call the Ojo. That is when a witch doctor has put a curse on a person. Most people die when they have been cursed by the witch doctor. We prayed for the little girl. She had been lying unconscious for two weeks on their floor. Her mother was awakened that night by bright lights that lit up the whole hut. In the jungle it is so dark at night that you cannot even find your own hand in front of your face. It gives a whole new meaning to darkness. She saw two men. One shone so brightly that you could not see his face. He knelt down and touched the little girl's forehead. The little girl's mom worshiped God for the rest of the night. She knew that they had been visited by Jesus the Healer. The next day her little girl woke up starving and wanted to go out and play. She has been healed ever since!

Then there was a little girl who was born with autism. She never came out of her autistic world. When she would wake up she was in a violent seizure. They took the little girl to the witch doctor most of her life. He could not heal her. She was 6 years old at this time. The pastor's wife was awakened in the night. She prayed all night and then the Lord told her to go over to the house of the little girl. She went over to the house and asked the parents if she could pray for the little girl who had been in a seizure for two weeks. The doctor told them that she would die of a heart attack if she did not come out of the seizure soon. They were not Christians.

The pastor's wife followed the instructions of the Lord which were to break the curse off of the little girl and then cast the devil out of her. When she did that, the seizures quit and the little girl lay still, as if she was dead. Then the little girl, who had never made one sound in her life, lay there with her eyes open. The pastor's wife touched the little girl's throat and asked God to heal the voice box in the little girl. The little girl began to cry out loud for the first time in her life. Everyone in the village cried that day because they knew that God had visited them personally and had healed the little girl.

The father ran into the jungle and cried hysterically for three days and nights. You could hear him all over the village. On the fourth day he asked the pastor to pray for him to accept Jesus in his life. When he was water baptized, it was so emotional. He dropped to his knees crying and thanking God for touching his little girl's life. He has never missed a church service since then. The little girl has never gone back into the autism world nor has she had a seizure.

One night the pastor came to get us for an emergency in the village. We arrived at the village and a young boy was dead. He had gone with his father, Nelson, to cut trees. When the boys turn 12 years old they go with their dad to learn to use the chainsaw to cut trees. Everything was going good until the wind blew in and the tree fell the wrong way. The boy did not know which way to run. The tree fell on him and he was flat as a pancake. It was awful! Nelson carried his son for three hours on his back. The tradition of the Indians is when a child dies, the father digs a hole and buries the child alone. Nelson blamed himself and soon was on his deathbed. He had a bleeding ulcer and the doctors only gave him a few months to live.

We were in church one night and Dennis was preaching. Nelson went outside to vomit blood. He failed to come back so his wife and a few women went out to see what had happened to him. He appeared to be dead. He had no vital signs. We stopped and prayed for him. When we got him to the clinic the doctor told us that he had slipped into a coma and would die that night. The next morning I came to check on him and he was sitting up in a chair waiting for me. I was so shocked and then he began telling me what had happened to him. When he went out of the church he needed to vomit. After he vomited he was caught up in the heavenlies. Jesus stood at the gate and He looked through the windows of heaven. Jesus said, "Nelson, look at your son. He is whole and he is so happy." Nelson was instantly healed when he saw his son's body completely restored. Needless to say we had many crusades with Nelson telling his testimony!

Nelson had accepted the Lord about five years before this happened. He was Spirit-filled and used of God mightily with his testimony of God's goodness. He renounced the call of the passing of the mantel of the witch doctor. From very young they are selected and taught how to work in the supernatural. The witch doctor that had trained him from a child died. The witch doctor mantel came upon Nelson from the grave and he accepted it. Today he works against the gospel.

Another time there was a lady who had several children. Her husband ran off and left them. If my memory serves me right, she had five children including a baby of six months. A group of teens was visiting at that time and one of the teenagers asked me about her. I told him the story and he said, "I have such a burden for her."

A couple of days went by and he still could not sleep for the burden he had for this lady. So the teens took up an offering and gave it to her after one of the night crusades. She gave this testimony upon receiving the offering: "I told the Lord that unless something happens today I am going to cook the baby and we can eat him tonight." They had not eaten in three weeks, if I remember right. The teenager was so glad that he was obedient to the Lord! I saw that lady some time later and she had remarried and all the kids were doing well. She told me that she would never forget the kindness of those teenagers and how the Lord supernaturally saved her baby.

There was another child born in the village who kept bleeding from her ears. They took her to the doctor and the doctors told the parents that they had never seen such bad ears. Her tubes were blocked with infection and they were pretty sure even when the infection cleared up that the child would be deaf. Her parents prayed and believed God. The child was healed and her hearing is perfect!

THE CLINIC

During this time the doctor at the only clinic in the jungle asked us for help. They had no car and needed transportation to the city for the severe cases. We worked with the clinic for around seven  years. At that time it took us 10 hours to get into Panama City which was only 90 miles away. You had to have a four-wheel-drive vehicle to get through the mud and rough terrain.

We became close friends with the doctors in the clinic over the years. Many of the doctors were not Christians, but they saw so many miracles that many gave their hearts to the Lord during that time.

The government of Panama has socialized medicine. They pay for your medical training, but then you owe them five years of your life to repay them for your training. They send these doctors into the jungles. They have no medicine and no equipment to help them care for the people. They are devastated because so many people die that could have been saved if they only had some medicine and equipment.

The saddest case I had ever seen was when a man was getting off a bus with his family. Another man driving a pickup truck going the opposite direction was traveling pretty fast. The roads were all dirt, and in the dry season there is so much dust that it is hard to see. The family went to cross the street and ran right into the path of the pickup truck. There was a man riding a horse on the side of the street and his little boy was following behind him. They had just harvested their first crop and were taking it to the market to sell. When the pickup truck saw the people who had gotten off the bus, he swerved to the side of the road to keep from hitting them as they crossed the road. He hit the man on the horse and cut both of his legs off. Two of the people crossing the road were pronounced dead onsite. Another man broke his back. We were asked to transport everyone to the clinic.

The man riding the horse kept screaming out with pain, but he bled to death. He and his son had come to the jungle and bought a piece of land. They were going to plant and harvest the first crop and then send for the rest of their family who lived up by the Costa Rican border. The little boy listened to his father scream with pain all night until he finally died. The hospital walls were full of blood where he had bled to death. It took them two weeks to find the family of the little boy.

Needless to say the doctor was devastated. He felt so helpless. He cried in Dennis's arms for hours. Having medical training, Dennis could understand his frustration.

FROM CLINIC TO HOSPITAL

We prayed with the doctor and together we believed God to build the clinic into a 48-bed operational hospital. We petitioned the government for vaccination programs in all of the villages and started fighting disease that killed so many young children before their first birthday. The Indians did not trust white man's medicine, but if we went with the doctors then they would let them do just about anything. We helped them vaccinate babies all over the jungle. Our years of hard work building relationships had paid off.

One time we brought a man to the clinic who had cholera. Cholera is very contagious. We had to set up an area outside where we could quarantine him. By the time we got the epidemic under control, cholera had spread to about 20 people. They were coming from everywhere. Most of them had walked for days and were very dehydrated. Dehydration is your worst enemy when dealing with cholera and malaria. Over the years our children were exposed to just about all the diseases in the jungle. We took them everywhere with us and not one time were they ever sick or even have any of the symptoms of the diseases.

Malaria is something that you deal with a lot in the jungle. It is carried by a mosquito, so it is almost impossible to fight. You can be injected with some of the disease to help your body build up a resistance to it, but it doesn't guarantee that you will not get it. There was no way they could spray the entire jungle to kill the mosquitoes that carried it. They did, however, begin to go house to house and spray our houses. Most people lived in grass huts and had a lot of water caught in water containers. They caught rain water off of their roofs to drink and facilitate their needs. Mosquitoes nest in water, so we had to keep all water tanks covered so they could not get inside. A water purification system was started in which you put a cap of bleach into a 55-gallon barrel of water. This system really worked to purify the water. It was not too pleasant to drink, but it sure was better than parasites or amebas.

We went home to visit our supporting churches and they put us in contact with a medical mission's warehouse. We were able to furnish the hospital with all of the medical machines and beds that they needed. We purchased all of the machines and beds for $10,000. The equipment was valued at about $200,000.

The hospital has come a long way since then. Today people from all over the jungle come there for medical attention. While we were gone, the German government paid for the one-room clinic to be turned into a 48-bed fully operational hospital. They had never been given such a large amount of money and recognized it as a miracle.

We saw God work so many miracles while we were transporting people who were critically injured to the city.

I particularly remember a baby being born that weighed two pounds. The mother was a member of one of the churches. The baby's name was Benjamin. The doctor told us that they both would probably die on the way into town. The mother was hemorrhaging, so he was not sure she would make it. We prayed with her, and she and her son are alive today.

When the clinic was given an ambulance we no longer worked that much with them. When we could we still took patients to Panama City. One lady had a tubal pregnancy and lost her baby. They could not get her to quit bleeding. We took her into Panama. The doctor sent a nurse with us because he fully expected her to die on the way. She was a sister in the Lord and asked us to pray with her and so we did before we left for the treacherous ten-hour four-wheel-drive trip. When we arrived at the hospital emergency room she was in critical condition and had lost one-third of the blood in her body. They gave us a very negative report and said she would die real soon. They began giving her blood throughout the night. The next morning the doctors said they thought she would miraculously make it after all and not die. She returned to the Darien in three days perfectly healed!

I remember one of the policemen had a little boy bitten by a deadly poisonous fer-de-lance snake. You usually have three hours after you have been bitten. There was no antivenom in the jungle. With 48 different types of deadly snakes, they did not feel they needed it. Most people do not see the snake that bites them so you cannot give medicine for an unknown poisonous snake. You have to know exactly what kind of snake bites you for the medicine to work.

Another policeman's wife had a severe heart attack. We took her to Panama City and she is alive and well today.

Our position as the ambulance drivers helped us build very strong relationships with everyone in the jungle including the police force.

This phase of our lives ended when the government started recognizing the needs of the jungle. Today we donate things on a regular basis to the hospital, but we no longer are actively involved with it. The Indians trust the doctors to come in their villages without us now so we no longer accompany them. Part of our hearts will always be with the doctors and nurses at that clinic/hospital. We went through a lot together and it built a strong bond between us.

MONEY IN THE JUNGLE

We began working with the government to put schools and an immunization program in Darien. Today every village has a school up to the sixth grade. It is expensive for the children to go to school because of the uniforms. It costs around $200 a year for the uniforms and all of the materials that they need to go to school. The schools' lessons are taught in Spanish. Most of the children only spoke their dialect so that was a real adjustment. Spanish is spoken fluently in most of the villages today. The children all wear the national uniform and shoes to school.

Basically there was no money. The Indians were farmers and grew enough for their families and had no need of money. Things have changed today. They grow enough to sell to the markets in Panama City. Every village, no matter how deep in the jungle they are, has an immunization program to vaccinate their children. This has decreased the infant mortality from around 65% to around 10%.

Social medicine here costs $2 to see a doctor. Sometimes they have the medicine but most of the time they do not, so they have to buy the medicine in a nearby pharmacy. The medicine is very expensive so most people do not buy it. The children have to have a complete physical before they go to school and also a dental checkup. No one can start school with a cavity.

We taught a lot of classes on hygiene to cut down on disease. For instance, one time I taught a class on what to do when a mother's milk dries up. This is a real problem for them because they have a baby every year. The clinic taught me the class and then I taught it to the mothers.

The clinic suggested that the women wear brassieres. We worked with the American military, and their PX gave us a big box of brassieres that did not sell that year. I had a group coming in so I just sent the box into the village, telling the chief that the ladies knew what these were for!

I brought a group of pastors in there to hold a crusade. The Indian ladies were all lined up with their bras on. They were so proud of them! The pastors looked at me kind of strange but never asked me about it. To this day when the ladies are going to dress up or have their pictures taken they run and put their bras on!

They began going to the doctor when the kids would get sick. All of this takes money. They did not have any at that time. I asked the Lord to help me find a way to help them financially. It cost about $200 per child to send them to school. He gave me a fantastic idea. I noticed that they were very good at making baskets. They needed a little help on cleanliness but the designs were excellent. So I brought in a man, Lynn Brockman, to teach them how to make cleaner baskets. He had previously worked for the Peace Corps. He taught the Indians how to make their baskets clean and to be more creative in their designs. I bought them a book on Indian designs. Each family chose one design and no one else could make that design. Lynn also taught them to carve wooden animals from the Cocobolo tree. He introduced them to the Tagua nut and taught them how to carve it. They make beautiful carvings of animals out of it.

I began a basket club and started selling their baskets and carvings to the American military. The Indians began to be able to afford to send their kids to school and to take them to the doctor. They now have sufficient money to meet all of their needs.

SPECIAL GRACE

In 1993 American missionaries were kidnapped in the jungle. All the mission organizations withdrew their American missionaries. Our mission board told us to be free to follow the Lord. Dennis said, "The devil didn't send me and the devil isn't going to run me off." So we stayed. We became the only American missionaries in the jungle for many years.

All of the young pastors started to come to Dennis for counseling. We were older than most of them so they looked to us for wisdom. We became very close friends with them. During this time Dennis formed a confraternity to unite pastors and began having a conference every three months to encourage the young pastors.

Because we chose to stay we were in a lot of danger. The United States president strongly advised all American citizens to get out of Panama. If we chose to stay then we were on our own.

One night when we were coming home from Panama City the border police stopped us. This was normal procedure but this time there was a young policeman who asked us to get out of the car. He took our passports and asked us to step around to the side of the building. When the senior policeman saw him taking us around to the side of the building he came running out of the building to reprimand the young policeman. He said, "What are you doing?" The young policeman said, "We were given orders to kill all Americans  that come through this border." The senior policeman said, "Don't you know who these people are?" He said, "I do not care who they are. I am not disobeying orders. If I do, Noriega will have me killed."

The senior policeman stood between us and the younger policeman. About that time many of the older policemen came over and they, too, stood in front of us. The senior policeman said, "If you are going to kill them, then your bullets will have to go through us first. These people are the ambulance drivers here in the jungle. If it were not for them, my child would have died." The other policemen shared of times we took either them or their loved ones into the city. The senior policeman took our passports away from the lower-ranking policeman and gave them back to us and said, "Get you and your family in the car, Dennis. We never saw you tonight."

That night I could not sleep. I knew the stakes were getting very high. The Lord asked me if I would be willing to die for the gospel. I wrestled with it for a while but thought, "We do not have anything else in life that we love like the work of the Lord." I finally said, "Yes, Lord, I would be willing to give my life for the gospel." Then He said, "Would you be willing to give the lives of your children for the gospel?" I was devastated by the question. For two weeks I wrestled with this question. I knew it was very much a reality that this could happen.

We asked the kids if they wanted to go home and live with their grandparents until the danger was over. None of them wanted to leave. We explained how dangerous it could get but none of them wanted to leave. I went back to the Lord and told Him I could not give the lives of my children for the gospel. I was very aware of how Noriega killed families. He would tie the boys up and if their parents denied Jesus then he would let them go. If they did not, he would have them shot in the head. I thought since it was quick maybe I could be strong enough to not deny Jesus. They would not suffer. But the thing that I could not get out of my mind was how he killed young girls. He would have all the soldiers sexually molest her in front of you as she was screaming out for help. All you had to do was deny Jesus to stop the pain. I just did not know if I could be strong enough to watch Jennifer going through such torture and stand for Jesus until they killed her. The Lord told me, "Jeanne, do you know what got Me through Calvary? That was my only little boy they were beating so badly. When He fell the first time going up the hill I wanted to send 10,000 angels to get Him. But if I did I would seal the fate of all mankind for eternity. I had to turn away when He was hanging on the cross and calling out to Me to forgive them. At that moment a hush fell all over heaven. No one could believe that the innocent Lamb of God was being crucified. It was so unfair. He was so pure and without sin. He never did anything wrong in His whole life, yet He was sentenced to death. The thing that got Me through that night that He laid in the tomb was the fact that I knew He would be raised again and He would be in eternity forever with Me. The suffering was only for a moment in time, then I would have My son back again forever. That is what got Me through that night."

When He told me that, it seemed like a special grace dropped down upon me. I knew in my heart that it would never happen, but yet if it did, I would be prepared. His grace would cover me and make me strong. ·

The Lord had to deal with me about this because my greatest fear in moving to the jungle was that I would lose one of the children. After I went through that time of decision, nothing fazed me. I just seemed to be so brave.

Many times after that the police would bombard our house in the middle of the night and demand to see our papers. They would always apologize before they left, saying they were just following orders but sure hated it.

They threw Dennis in jail from time to time. One time they kept him for three days. I did not know where he was. I just knew he was three days late coming home. He was out evangelizing when they took him. He said they told him after the three days that they needed a ride to the port. The port road divided into a fork at one point and everyone knew if they told you to go left that they were going to kill you and throw your body in the river. When he got to this point they told him to go right. He had a plan in mind of what he was going to do to escape if they told him to turn left. Thank God it never happened!

One time they threw our middle son in jail. The kids were given special driving permits to take workers back and forth to the farm. A new policeman stopped Jason when he was taking workers home. He asked for his license. When Jason showed him the permit the policeman said it was illegal. Our son told him that the chief of police in the jungle granted it. They took him to jail and he spent the night with people who were in there for murder. It shook him up pretty badly. The next day the chief of police came and let him out of jail. He told Jason to tell us that he was sorry but he was out of town when this happened.

We had several close calls but God always protected us!

OPPOSITION IN A NEW CHURCH

During this time Dennis was also pioneering a new church in a village called Puerta Lara.

After one year he began a two-year Bible school. He walked twice a week into the village, eight miles each way. He would teach four hours a day and then walk out. He did this for two years.

This village holds a special place in my heart because it is the first village that I visited with Dennis in the jungle. It was in this area that we almost died, lost in the ocean in shark-infested areas.

The village could not be reached by jeep for nine months of the year because the path would wash out and become impassable. During the three months that we could drive in there, Dennis began holding crusades. The other nine months he either walked (eight miles one way) or rode a horse or went by canoe.

I remember seeing my little blonde-haired boy there and thinking, "You were the little boy that God used to bring us here."

This village is a port town. A lot of loggers and drug dealers ran drugs through the jungle and would stop at that port. Needless to say, they had a big impact on the people there.

There was a big spiritual power struggle in that village with the witch doctors. Five witch doctors lived in this small village of about 400 people. They were constantly challenging the power of God within us. One of the witch doctors there was said to be one of the most powerful witch doctors in the jungle. There were all kinds of stories about him. I believed them because he, along with all of the witch doctors, seemed to be full of death. When you looked into their eyes you seemed to be looking into the pit of hell. They were evil and intentionally killed people. It showed in their eyes.

Not all witch doctors are evil. Some of them wanted to help people and got into the business because of that desire. When they hear the gospel they are very easily converted. It is the ones with the evil intentions that challenge you on everything. The crusades were more powerful in that village because God is always proving that He has the ultimate power.

One of the crusades had a lot of opposition. The crusade had been planned for one week. Dennis had to walk into the village which was an eight-hour walk one way because the road was not passable. All week the Indians would come to our tent and tell us of all kinds of manifestations of the devil trying to persuade the people not to go to the crusade.

One told this story: There was an old man with white hair that would visit the village years ago. He would come riding on the river on a towel. When he got off the towel on the bank he would shake out the towel and use it as a shirt on his back. When it was time to bathe he would take the shirt off and shake it out again and it became a towel to dry with. He had many miraculous signs, and the people believed everything that he said. We know now that he taught them the doctrine of devils. He had not visited our village for one generation until this time. All of the elders in the village remember when he used to visit on a regular basis but none of this generation had ever seen him.

He came to visit them that week. He shook out his towel and spat on the ground. He said this generation had not followed his teachings and therefore he was putting a curse on the village. He said if they went to the crusade this weekend, the curse would be a permanent curse on each person who attended. He said that there would always be sickness in the village, their babies would be born like monkeys, their crops would always fail no matter how hard they worked, and there would be no unity in the village. He shook out the towel and rode off over the waters. He has never been seen since. It terrified the people.

Another group of people came to our property and shared another testimony. They said that they were walking along and a drunken man came riding up on a donkey. The donkey talked and told them the same thing that the old man with white hair had said in the village.

Whenever there is a mighty manifestation of the power of the devil, you know God is going to do something miraculous. I could hardly wait until the crusade began. I was so anxious to see what God was going to do in that village!

In spite of all of this, the people came out to the crusade for miles around. It was so crowded that you could not get into the hut where it was being held. Dennis was very bold and taught on the scripture that says you can not serve two gods at the same time. You serve one God with all of your heart and mind and soul. You either believe in Jesus or you serve the devil.

The pigs and chickens were running through the pulpit area while he was preaching. He was so focused that he did not even notice the animal kingdom running wild within the meeting. Then a dog came up, hiked his leg, and urinated on Dennis's pant leg. Dennis kicked the dog and it went out running and screaming. Dennis continued like nothing had happened. The anointing was so strong it was captivating. He preached for three hours and no one moved. It was awesome!

In that village there was a young girl, about 19 years old, who was a raving maniac. Every night she would rip her clothing off and run stark naked throughout the village screaming like she was being tormented in her mind. She had done this for years. During that crusade she came in totally dressed and healed. She was bathed and her hair was combed. The people were astonished and knew that something had happened to the young girl.

She told of how she would listen to the gospel that Dennis preached, and in one of the classes he taught on redemption. She cried out to God to redeem her from this torment in her mind. She said she was instantly delivered and conformed into a new person. She knew without a doubt that God had heard her cry and had touched her life. The people sat there and were astonished at the transformation of this young girl's life.

She told that when she was 12 years old she was having female problems. Her mom took her to a doctor who told her that she could never have children. They believe children are a sign of God's blessings on your life. The voices began tormenting her every night and would tell her it was better to be dead than to be barren. They told her no one would ever marry a barren woman and God had cursed her life forever. She said when she heard Dennis's lesson on redemption she knew what the voices had told her was a lie. She began speaking to the voices and taking authority over them. Today she is married with three children.

Time and time again people made a decision to live for the one true God and to renounce the ways of the devil. There were many people healed and set free that night.

The people were convinced that the visit from the elderly white-headed man was a lie and they did not have to accept the curse that he put on the village.

That next day one of the witch doctors burned all of her paraphernalia in a big fire in front of the whole village to prove that she had chosen to serve the one true God. Usually when a witch doctor gets born again they burn all of their paraphernalia.

The first pastor Dennis put into the church was poisoned by one of the members of the church. A lady who had been a fifth-generation witch had gotten born again. She wanted her husband to be the pastor of the church. Even though she was born again the devil lived very much in her thoughts and actions. She poisoned the pastor and his wife and their five children with turtle meat. We sent them to Panama City to get medical help. After being in the hospital and almost dying, they chose to settle in the city.

The woman was tried by Indian court and sentenced to death. Her husband begged for her life, so she was given a choice of death or never returning to the jungle again. Her husband chose that they would leave. To this day she has never been back to the jungle.

Dennis began pastoring the church again until he could get another trained pastor in it.

I remember one lady who was in her late forties who got pregnant. I believe this was her tenth child. When she was seven months pregnant the doctor told her that he could not find the heartbeat of the baby. He suggested that she go into Panama City for more testing. When she got there they told her that the baby was dead inside of her. They suggested that she abort the baby. She said, "No! My God will heal the baby." She came back to the Darien. The doctors told her the baby would poison her body if she did not abort it soon. She refused and said, "You will see this baby is going to be born healthy and whole." She carried the baby the full nine months. She was  alone in the house when the baby was born, a little girl, alive and very healthy. She had been dead by all medical tests for two months. This is probably the most amazing miracle that I have ever seen. The mother took her to the clinic for her baby shots. The doctor confirmed that the baby's life was a miracle. She named her Carolina.

God has done and is still doing many miracles in that village.

PASTOR JOSÉ

We have had several pastors in that church. The last one has been a tremendous man of God. He has pastored the church for more than 15 years now. The church has really grown and we have built another cement block church to accommodate the growing congregation.

Pastor José operates in the gifts of miracles in his everyday life.

I remember when a little boy fell from a tree and broke his arm. José laid hands on him and the whole village heard the bones popping and going back into place. The arm was badly deformed, but after being prayed for, it was completely normal. He went back out and played.

A man who was bitten by a snake was given up to die. He went to the clinic and was sent to Panama City where they told him that the poison of the snake was too advanced in his body and he would die on the way home. He went back to the doctor in the jungle and they had someone take him home. They suggested that he see a witch doctor. When he got there he was taken to the witch doctor's house. The witch doctor waited until the moon was full and then he took his hands and put them on the inside of the man's body and pulled out a set of snake fangs. The man was instantly healed, but he had to sell his soul to the devil to keep his healing. Pastor José prayed for him and he gave his soul to Jesus and is still healed today!

In this village there were four witch doctors, one of which was very powerful. This particular witch doctor had tried every way that he could to ruin our pastor. Pastor José is a man that walks in an incredible amount of love. His love just keeps on and keeps on, and eventually the people repent and give their hearts to Jesus. When Pastor José heard that the witch doctor who had persecuted him so badly was dying in the clinic, he went to visit him. Of course, the witch doctor was ashamed because he could not heal himself. The doctors said they could not find anything wrong with him but his major organs were shutting down. They only gave him a few hours to live. Pastor José asked if he could pray for the witch doctor. He was so mad that Pastor José came to visit him, but he finally said okay. When Pastor José prayed for him, he was instantly healed and released from the hospital. Of course, it was a really big sign of who held the highest power!

Another time a man named Tiliano fell out of a tree in that village. He fell on his back from about 50 feet in the air. When he hit the ground he missed a rock by about an inch that would instantly have killed him. I was at the clinic when they brought him in. They had carried him for 15 miles to get him there. He was unconscious. The doctors said he had internal injuries and sent him to Panama City.

Pastor José could not leave the village so he sent a note to Tiliano, encouraging him to believe God for total healing. We took the note to Tiliano in Panama City. He read the note and cried. Dennis prayed for him. He said, "Dennis, I am going to walk out of here a healed man." Dennis encouraged him to keep believing.

The next day we met with the doctors and they told us that he had severed his spinal cord and would never walk again. There was a large opening in his spine where it was separated. Tiliano kept telling everyone in the hospital that he was going to walk out of there a healed man. He was in a ward of six other men who had been severely hurt.

One night he said he saw a light come into the room. The light caused a warm feeling, like a healing balm, to go all throughout his body. He had not walked in two weeks. He could not even get up to use the toilet. They had to carry him everywhere. He jumped up out of bed and ran down the hallway. It was the middle of the night, so he woke everyone up in the hospital. When he got back to the ward the other men began to cry. The man next to him had been in a car accident and they were going to amputate his leg because it was crushed beyond repair. That man said, "I do not know your God, but do you think He would heal me?" Tiliano said, "I am sure that He would if you asked Him to." He led the man in the prayer of salvation and could hear all kinds of muscles moving and bones cracking. The man's leg was totally restored. He jumped up and ran all over the ward!

There was another man in the ward who had fallen out of a tree. His legs were bent around his body and up over his shoulders. They tried everything but could not get the legs to relax and come down in their right position. When Tiliano prayed for him, the legs came down and he was totally healed!

There were four instant healings in that ward that night. All the men got up and started packing their things. They all checked out of the hospital that night. Tiliano lived in the jungle so he just spent the night. He planned on leaving the next day.

The doctor came in the next morning and said, "I heard something happened in this ward last night." Tiliano said, "Yes, we had a visitation from God." The doctor said, "I am going to take an MRI today and we will just see if you are truly healed or if this all in your head. Sometimes things happen like this but it is only for a short time." When he took the MRI he came back and said, "I do not know what happened to you, but there is not even a scar where your spine was severed. You are a healed man." Needless to say, when Tiliano went home the village went wild and many people rededicated their lives over the miracle they saw in his body.

A child in the village grew increasingly ill. He was taken to the doctors who said the child was dying, but they couldn't find anything wrong with him even though his body was definitely shutting down. The boy was prayed for and instantly healed!

There was a little girl born with acute asthma. She was 5 years old and never had lived a normal life as a child. She seemed to have one asthma attack after another. She was not a member of the church. The little girl's parents sent for Pastor José and asked him to come to the clinic because the little girl was dying. When he arrived she was under oxygen, but the doctor said she would not live through the night. The parents said that they had never gone to his church but they knew that they believed in healing. They asked if he would pray for their little girl. Pastor José laid hands on her and he said he felt virtue going out of him into the little girl's body. The little girl looked up at him and smiled. The doctors came back in and said that they wanted to take her off of the oxygen. When they did, she jumped up totally healed! She is doing well today and has never had another asthma attack. Needless to stay her whole family goes to church and are strong Christians!

A man was diagnosed as having an incurable blood disease. He did not know the Lord. He asked Pastor José to come pray for him because he was dying and wanted to get right before his maker. When Pastor José arrived, the whole family was there. It was obvious that the man was dying. Pastor José knelt down to the floor where the man was laying. He said "You don't have to die. You can live if you want to." The man looked up at him and said he would really like to live but was too sick. Pastor José said, "Let's pray and ask God to heal your body." When he prayed for the man, it was like electricity hit the man and he jumped up to his feet and began running all around. He was instantly healed! He and his whole family accepted the Lord and are faithfully serving the Lord today.

The church is very strong today and continues to see miracles regularly.

SUPERNATURAL PROTECTION

Dennis felt that this church was fully established so he began evangelizing deeper into the jungle with a group of his students. They would be gone about nine days at a time.

I told myself that I would be all right while he was gone. Every time he drove off in our jeep, fear would grip me. I would be reciting the scripture that says, *"For God hath not given us the spirit of fear; but of power, and of love, and of a sound mind"* (2 Timothy 1:7) as he left the muddy path of our farm.

The children and I did not travel with Dennis because they were still in school. It is very hard to travel and home-school, so I chose to stay home until they were out of high school.

Most missionaries send their kids to a boarding school. I just did not have the heart to do that. I thought no matter how hard it is they are better off with their parents. I had so many missionaries say it was an injustice to our children for them to be illiterate because of the call on our lives. I took home-schooling seriously and was a very strict teacher. I did not let them slide on anything. We began school at 9 a.m. and ended about 4 p.m. each evening.

While Dennis was gone I did really well during the days, but the nights seemed to be so long. I would quote the 91st Psalm out loud to the kids before they went to sleep. It was the Word that God spoke directly to my heart to calm all of my fears.

> *He that dwelleth in the secret place of the most High shall abide under the shadow of the Almighty.*
>
> *I will say of the LORD, He is my refuge and my fortress: my God; in him will I trust.*
>
> *Surely he shall deliver thee from the snare of the fowler, and from the noisome pestilence.*
>
> *He shall cover thee with his feathers, and under his wings shalt thou trust: his truth shall be thy shield and buckler.*
>
> *Thou shalt not be afraid for the terror by night; nor for the arrow that flieth by day;*
>
> *Nor for the pestilence that walketh in darkness; nor for the destruction that wasteth at noonday.*
>
> *A thousand shall fall at thy side, and ten thousand at thy right hand; but it shall not come nigh thee.*
>
> *Only with thine eyes shalt thou behold and see the reward of the wicked.*
>
> *Because thou hast made the LORD, which is my refuge, even the most High, thy habitation;*
>
> *There shall no evil befall thee, neither shall any plague come nigh thy dwelling.*
>
> *For he shall give his angels charge over thee, to keep thee in all thy ways.*
>
> *They shall bear thee up in their hands, lest thou dash thy*

foot against a stone.

Thou shalt tread upon the lion and adder: the young lion and the dragon shalt thou trample under foot. (In this part I also added tigers and black panthers!)

Because he hath set his love upon me, therefore will I deliver him: I will set him on high, because he hath known my name.

He shall call upon me, and I will answer him: I will be with him in trouble; I will deliver him, and honour him.

With long life will I satisfy him, and show him my salvation.

PSALM 91

That psalm I hid in my heart and it never failed to protect us and keep us.

During this time I really grew in the things of the Lord. I could no longer ride on Dennis's faith. It was me and the Lord from here on out. I was so thankful that I had gone to Bible school, too, and that I had a strong foundation in the Bible to rely on.

One night we were lying in the tent and I felt something brush up against my body. Whatever it was, it was big and very long. It began to growl. I laid there thinking of what it could be. The fur was too smooth to be a wild pig, and it did not sound like a pig. It was too short to be a deer. Besides, deer do not growl. It could not be a coyote because it was too small. It could not be a saino because their fur is like a porcupine. It could not be a margay (a small bobcat) because it was too small and their growl sounds more like a pet cat.

All of a sudden I realized what it was! I looked out of one of the holes in the tent and, sure enough, it was a tiger about five feet long. The moon was full that night and I could see him clearly. He was large and acted hungry. I began reciting the 91st Psalm so loud that I woke all of the kids! The tiger circled the tent about five times. We remained still and put our confidence in the power of God's Word to keep us safe.

After about 40 minutes, the tiger left. He left our tent, but he did not leave the area. I could hear him for nights circling around the land.

One of the things that the Indians taught us was that when a tiger is growling he will not attack. He is trying to get his prey to run. If you run, then he attacks. If you stand still, he will respect you and never attack you.

I know that is true because one time Dennis was walking into a village six hours from our house. Night fell and a tiger began following him. Dennis said the tiger followed him for six hours. He said he knew if he kept the same pace the tiger would not attack. He was so close Dennis could feel his paws rumble the earth behind him. When he arrived at the village where there were several campfires, the tiger took off. They are deathly afraid of fire.

> *He shall cover thee with his feathers, and under his wings*
> *shalt thou trust: his truth shall be thy shield and buckler.*

PSALM 91:4

I found that there was nothing as faithful as the Word of God to protect us in the jungle. At that time we were not allowed to own a gun so our confidence was 100% in the Word of God to protect us.

While we were alone we learned to speak to the clouds so they would rain and we would have drinking water. We learned to speak to storms and tell them not to strike us or anything around us. We learned to speak to the water in the ocean and command the waves to settle down. A great calm came over the water every time.

I learned how faithful God was to protect us and to take care of us. His Word brought peace to my soul and would calm me down in every situation.

ALTO PLYONA

The next village that Dennis pioneered a church in was called Alto Plyona. We never went into a village unless we were invited.

Dennis pioneered this church that could only be reached five

months of the year by a four-wheel-drive jeep. It was a five-hour walk into the village. The village was way back in an area that had been cut down and burned, so you were exposed to the scorching sun that gets up to 120 degrees during the day. Tigers run in that land and howler monkeys, very accurate coconut-throwing monkeys. The howler monkeys are very territorial. When you come into their area they throw everything at you. The most dangerous things they throw are coconuts, which could kill a person if they hit you in the head. You had to walk consistently and quietly so they knew you were only passing through. If anyone ran, the coconuts would begin to fall.

During this time of pioneering the church, Noriega, the dictator of Panama, had national elections. They were always rigged to make sure that he would get in office again. He would send buses to the Darien and demand everyone to come in to the city and vote for him. It was mandatory and no questions were to be asked.

The Indians in Alto Plyona refused to go and vote for him. Not too long after the elections were held a helicopter landed near the village. Noriega's soldiers, called the dignity squad, got out of the helicopter and robbed the village, taking everything including the rifles and the ammunition used to hunt. They took the food that was stored for the year and the seed to replant for next season. The people were left to die for not voting for Noriega.

The people began to cry out to God for help. The next morning Indians from all the villages could be seen walking on the road to Alto Plyona. Everyone was carrying food. Even the small four-year-old children were carrying sugar or flour or rice. They came from all over the Darien. When they arrived in Alto Plyona, the people ran out to meet them. The people asked, "Have you come because you have heard that Noriega's men robbed us of everything?" They said, "No, we have not heard of anything like that. We are here because the Lord woke us up in the night and told us that there was an emergency in Alto Plyona. He said to leave right away and bring as much food as we could carry."

The chief of the village of Rio Cito happened to be in Alto Plyona when Noriega's men came in. He was there when the village united in prayer asking for God's help. It was such a sign to him that God would hear the cries of people so far away and send help for them. He asked whose church they were members of. They told him that the founder of their church was Dennis Cook.

The chief of Rio Cito and several of his people walked out with the

Indians who had carried the food in to the village. On the way out, one of our pastors was bitten by a deadly poisonous snake. Normally you have 30 minutes before you die when you have been bitten by that snake. The unbelievers began to tease him and said, "You are going to die!" The pastor said, "No! I will not die because God needs me to preach the gospel to my people." He was sweating and could hardly walk, but when they reached their destination he was totally 100% healed! The unbelievers and the chief of Rio Cito had never seen anything like that before. The chief came to our home and invited Dennis in to his village to begin a work. Neither he nor any of his people had ever heard of Jesus.

When Dennis had established the church in Alto Plyona, he put a pastor in it and went on to establish a church in Rio Cito.

RIO CITO

Rio Cito means "little river" in English and is nine and a half hours by canoe through some of the densest parts of the Darien Jungle.

In Rio Cito Dennis had to have two translators speaking in both of the dialects. When he  was preaching he began speaking in tongues for over an hour. He had never done that before in any meeting. The people in Rio Cito never heard of Jesus. They had no idea who Jesus was or what He did for them. They all grew up in witchcraft, so that is what they believed in. After Dennis preached in tongues for over an hour, all of the people flocked to the altar. We found out later that he spoke fluently in their language!

He told a story in their language that was an ancient story and only the elders knew. That night he told a story about an ant who looked down from heaven and saw the other ants trying to build an anthill. They could not get it right so he came down from heaven to teach them how to build it. He died showing them the way.

It was a sign to all of the elders. They asked Dennis where he had heard that story. He told them that he made it up. Dennis is known for his crazy stories that just come to him as he is preaching. They told him that it was an ancient story only known by the elders in the village.

They knew that they could trust him because he knew the story.

The church in Rio Cito has seen many miracles. One of the royal family members could not have children. Medically they said that she was barren. We had a group of teenagers in at that time from Teen Mania and one of their leaders prayed for her. The barren lady conceived and has several children today.

Then there was a young woman who was kept locked in a room because she was mentally insane. Two of the teenagers went in the room to pray for the woman. She was instantly healed and is sane today and lives a normal life.

In the really remote areas they believe and trust in the Lord for everything. The doctors are days away, so they trust in the Lord. It is a way of life for them to be totally dependent on the Lord for all of their needs to be met.

When the church in Rio Cito was established, Dennis put a pastor in it.

TORTUGA

Then Dennis began to establish another church in a village called Tortuga, which means "turtle" in English.

This church is eight and a half hours away by canoe. It is

extremely primitive.

In this village you see a lot of tiger-teeth jewelry. Tigers run in that area because of its density. There are also wild boars and mountain pigs, and exotic birds fly in the sky there. You have to be careful when canoeing because of the large alligators that live in the river. It is a rule among the Indians that you never travel that river at night because of the alligators. They told horror stories of the alligators jumping up and eating someone in their canoe.

The Indians had never heard of Jesus in that village either. Dennis went in the village, building a relationship with them and the chief for about one year. When the Indians knew that they could trust him, they let him do whatever he wanted in the village. He did not preach until that time.

It took him three years to establish the church in that village.

We love working with teenagers and youth groups. Teen Mania is an organization that we have worked with for years. The kids are just awesome!

We brought a group of Teen Mania kids into that village. We let them do the drama about salvation so they were the first ones to preach the gospel in that village. An Indian lady sitting next to me said that was a really good story and asked if they had any more. They had no clue that the gospel had just been preached!

They would let us pray for them but no one responded to the salvation call. They did ask a bunch of questions, though, about what it meant to be a sinner. We found out later that deep in the jungle every night the oldest man in the thatched-roof home told stories until the children fell asleep. They thought we were just telling a wonderful story.

In their culture the older men are considered the wisest men in the village because they have lived longer than anyone else. No one ever laughed or criticized an older person. They were highly respected. No one talked back to their parents and the children did not fight. The children were very happy children and shared everything with their younger brothers and sisters. To them having a little brother or sister was such a blessing. No one thought it was a burden to watch the younger brothers and sisters. It was an honor to them to be that responsible.

Dennis spent about six months teaching that we are born as sinners in this world. He taught them about covenant with God because all Indian tribes have covenants in their history. When they understood the message of our covenant with God, they all received the Lord.

As the church was being established, we brought another group of teens in the following year. There were 36 teens in my canoe alone. A tropical storm hit and the river raised 16 feet. A tree fell over the riverbed and Dennis and a few Indians got out of their canoes and chopped a hole in the tree large enough that we could get the canoes through.

When we went under the tree limbs that hung over the water, about 200 tarantulas jumped in our canoe. They were crawling all over our bodies. I told the kids to close their eyes and to concentrate on the words that I was speaking to them. I quoted several scriptures, but mainly the one on greater is He that is within me than he that is in the world!

As we came out on the other side, a deadly poisonous snake about six feet long fell into the canoe. Dennis saw it and was able to get a large pole and flick it out into the water far enough away that it could not get back into the canoe.

When everyone calmed down I taught the teens how to get the tarantulas off of the them. We took a machete and flipped them way out into the middle of the river. If you flipped them close to the canoe they just jumped back in. Tarantulas are known for being able to jump large distances. But we eventually got them off of us and out of our canoe.

The river was rising very high and we knew nightfall was quickly approaching. You never want to be on the river at night in the jungle. During the day the alligators and crocodiles sleep and are very docile on the riverbeds. At night they feed in the river. They will jump in your canoe and attack everyone.

We arrived in the village about 6 p.m. and it was really dark. God had protected us and kept us safe.

I got all of the teenagers settled in for the night. When I went to lay down to sleep I saw a man in the moonlight. He was mixing medicine against our group. He was obviously a witch doctor. The Lord told me to get up and check one of the sleeping bags. When I did, there was a deadly poisonous snake in it. The witch doctor's plan was that when the teen got in it he would be killed by the snake bite, which would destroy our trip there. I quickly got the snake out before the teen even knew it was there.

We had a medical clinic planned for that village with open-air crusades each night. People from everywhere would travel to get there. The next day while Dennis and the team were setting up the medical clinic I had a children's crusade. A church in the States had donated 400 hardback books on the miracles of Jesus.

The witch doctor who I had seen in the night came up to me and asked for one of the books. I did not want to give him one because I had not brought any extra. I had just enough for all of the children. But the Lord spoke to me and told me to give him one, so I did.

The next day we began the medical clinic. The witch doctor was the first in line to be seen by the doctor. No one knew that he was the witch doctor but Dennis and me. We looked at each other with amazement that a witch doctor would be in line to see a doctor. They are known for healing themselves and everyone else.

The clinic was set up so that you gave your name, then you moved down the line and saw the doctor. He would diagnose you and write a prescription out. Then you would go to the next area and receive your medicine. Next you would be prayed for.

When the witch doctor saw the doctor, the Spirit of the Lord came on the doctor. He asked the witch doctor if he was born again. The witch doctor said, "No, but I have to get born again today." Dennis was standing there and asked him why. He said, "I read a book that a lady gave me on the miracles of Jesus. In the night Jesus appeared to me and told me if I did not get born again today that I would burn in hell for eternity. I have lived in hell all of my life on this earth and I do not want to live in hell for eternity." So Dennis prayed with him and the man received Jesus in his heart!

The village people were very nervous and anxious about something, so Dennis asked the chief what was wrong. He told him that the man who just got saved was the most powerful witch doctor in all of Darien and Colombia.

That night the former witch doctor asked Dennis if he could give his testimony. Dennis does not usually let them because they want to brag about all of their previous powers, but he felt led to let this man share.

He said that he saw our group get in the canoes nine and a half hours away. He said every child of the Most High God has the name of Jesus written in blood on his forehead. A light goes out wherever they walk and dispels all of the darkness. He said when a child of the Most High God walks into a dark area, that light goes out and penetrates the darkness and a trumpet blows and a voice shouts, "Attention! A child of the Most High God is walking in the area." The deeper they go into the darkness the brighter the light gets, penetrating all of the dark crevices of the darkest point. The trumpet blows a second time and a voice rings out and shouts, "A child of the Most High God is walking in the area." The third time the trumpet blows and a voice shouts, "Attention! A child of the Most High God is in the area," and the light has penetrated every bit of darkness around it not leaving one area without light. The last cry that goes out penetrates the darkest of the darkest crevice. Anyone who is not serving God begins to tremble. The ones who are serving the devil begin to tremble also. They hope that the children of the Most High God do not know that they are bearers of the most powerful name in all of the universe, that at the mention of that name everything in three worlds has to bow in honor of that name, and that the Word of God coming out of the mouth of the righteous holds so much power it makes every circumstance and situation bow its knee. The born-again witch doctor said most children of the Most High God do not know their authority and are no threat to the darkness at all. But, when he saw Dennis in the canoe, he knew he was in trouble.

He had been trying to kill Dennis and his family for over eight years by sending his strongest curse out like a missile to Dennis's farm in Quebrada Honda. He told how the farm is guarded by tall men who stand so close to one another that their arms are locked together and you cannot see inside the farm. In the supernatural realm inside the farm a great light shines that penetrates all the darkness around it. The missiles would hit the men where their arms were crossed and come back on him seven times stronger. One time he began bleeding all over his body and thought he would die.

He knew that if he ever ran into Dennis face to face he would have to bow his knee to the God that Dennis served because Dennis knew that he bore the most powerful name in the entire universe, and he knew the power of the spoken Word of God. A witch doctor's power could not hold a candle to the power that lived inside Dennis as well as all Christians. That is why he gave his heart to Jesus and bowed his knee to the highest power in all three worlds.

His testimony changed my life forever.

This ends the third chapter of our lives. I hope it has blessed you as much as it has blessed me to see the power of God in full manifestation!

CHAPTER FOUR
"LORD, I DID NOT KNOW THAT IT WOULD BE SO HARD!"

W e prepared ourselves for our first visit to the United States since we moved to the jungle. We would be sharing with our supporting churches.

BACK IN THE USA

We had a real culture shock when we arrived in the United States. A friend of ours took the kids to a candy store and told them to pick out all that they wanted. The kids began to cry because there was such a variety that they did not know what to pick.

As we began traveling from church to church we were

overwhelmed by the beauty of hearing worship in our native language. I would go so often to the altar and just cry. I could not explain to anyone why I was crying because no one could relate to what we had been through, mainly the hardships and the massive amount of souls that still did not know Jesus. There did not seem to be a burden for souls there.

I took a bubble bath and wanted to stay there all day. It was wonderful! Water was in abundance and there was a real toilet! I wondered if the people realized what a blessing it was to have so much water. Our water was so scarce in the jungle that we allowed ourselves only two gallons each to clean up with at night to conserve it. There are no bathtubs anywhere in the jungle or Panama City. It was such a special gift to me from God.

The United States is so rich in many ways. We have so many Bibles in our homes that we do not use most of them. Across the world people do not have a Bible translated in their language. I began to have a bad attitude towards the churches and the people because I felt like they should do more than they were doing. Every missionary goes

FOOTSTEPS OF FAITH

through this, and several other stages, when they go home. In reality it is really demonic because no pastor wants to support someone that has an arrogant attitude. Most pastors do have a heart for souls and they are doing the best that they can in supporting missions.

We settled in our hearts not to take it as a personal rejection when people chose not to financially support us. The vision that God gave to us was a supernatural vision. Anyone connecting with that supernatural vision had to be spoken to by God. Not everyone is called to support our mission.

I remember we went back to Rhema, the Bible school that we attended and graduated from, and Dennis and I both cried through every meeting. To hear the Word of God spoken from someone else's mouth blessed us far beyond anything anyone could speak. We had heard the gospel preached a million times, but it was so very special this time. I guess it is how people in the jungle feel when they hear the gospel for the first time. How rich is God's Word and how it ministers to your weary soul! We were totally restored by the time we went back to Panama. We had a refreshing in our vision and were on fire once again.

Most missionaries go through many stages when they visit the United States. The first time home they cry the whole time. It is quite a culture shock. They are very thankful for everything and find it hard to understand the petty things that people fight over.

The second time home they are mad at the world and think no one cares about them. Usually their support is low and they need someone to reach out to them. No one can explain how hard it is on the foreign field to make things happen when there is no money. As a general rule, churches change the missionaries that they support every six months. It is a very competitive world in the church for the financial support.

We have been so blessed to have very good friends to do all of our booking of meetings before we go home to the States. That way we do not waste any time trying to get meetings. Pastor Greg and Terri Roe did this for us for over 15 years. We will always be very grateful for the time and the finances that they put into that wonderful blessing for us. Our daughter does it today.

Having been on the mission field since 1981, we still find it very hard to get into new churches. We have tried everything that we can imagine to get into new churches. For the new missionary it is very difficult to get a meeting in a new church. As your ministry grows you need to broaden your base of support.

It's been such an honor that Rhema has promoted our ministry over the years. Today we speak almost on a yearly basis in their world missions school. They give us exposure but they do not financially support us. We went on the mission field before Rhema Bible Church was established. The missionaries they support are sent out from their church. Most of the teachers there are personal friends of ours, and our stories about the missions field are shared in a lot of their classes and in hundreds of churches.

BUILDING RELATIONSHIPS

Even with all of that exposure and being known that well, we still have a hard time getting into the new churches. Sometimes this gets very frustrating for the missionary because all they can see are the faces of the people on the field who are depending on them to raise support. At one time we had 29 different departments that were outreaches in the jungle. It is just so hard to stretch the money around. Imagine having a major ministry and not being able to take up an offering. The foreign governments do not allow the missionaries to work. Basically you are solely dependent on the support that comes from the United States.

I know from a pastor's point of view that they get so many calls every week for itinerate missionaries to come in. They just cannot adopt all of them. There has to be a solution to this problem, some kind of networking system that helps missionaries fund the vision God has put on their hearts. More missionaries go home because of a lack of finances and discouragement than any other reason, but there are others.

One of the reasons that I have observed is that a lot of missionaries are not good communicators. They seldom send a newsletter or give an update of what is going on. People need to know that the financial support they send is appreciated.

Another thing that I have observed is that there is no personal relationship developed with the people who support you or with the pastors of the churches that support you. We have tried hard to become close friends with our financial supporters and pastors. On the field this is done by writing letters and keeping them informed. For years I would send a personal letter and a picture of one of the Indians whose life they helped touch.

We could not afford to put out a newsletter at that time so I wrote letters by hand and mailed them individually. The "Pony Express" here is sometimes good and most of the time bad. When they accumulate too much mail they have been known to throw it in the ocean and start fresh!

Then the time came when we could afford to send a newsletter. I tried to make it very personal and tell things that were interesting. I found that people loved pictures so they could put a face with whom you were talking. We started out with just one 8.5" x 11" sheet that was printed on both sides. After a while, we went to two 8.5" x 11" sheets and put it in the form of a magazine. We had more to say by that time! Today it is easier to communicate because of internet accessibility, but not everyone has it. We have a signal once in a while but we have to travel 5 hours to get a good signal.

The first few years on the mission field you are learning the language and this pretty much takes all your energy. Many supporters think that you can walk right in and begin to speak the language within six months. There are many divorces in language school. It is extremely hard unless you are gifted with the ability to learn a language. I once heard T. L. Osborn, world missionary evangelist, say that it takes five years to be fluent in any language. I have found that to be true.

Many supporters do not realize that you have to build relationships before you can begin preaching the Word. In the Indian culture we could not talk about why we had moved to the jungle for two years. During those two years we built very strong relationships with the people as Dennis met with the heads of the Indian carmaca. Sometimes he would spend as much as four hours just talking to them.

There are four chiefs that are the heads over all of the villages. Dennis is the only man that has been given permission to build a church within the Indian reservation. It was never given before Dennis met them and has never been given to any other man since. It takes time to build relationships like that. Dennis honors the laws of the villages. You are supposed to ask permission from the chief before you enter into the village. Dennis still asks after all of these years. Honoring their culture speaks very loud.

A SIDE STEP

I would like to take a little side step here and talk to pastors who support missionaries.

In the United States everything church-related has to first start with a strong personal relationship with members of your congregation. You build your church one person at a time. Here, the people do not care how much you know until they know how much you care. We had to build relationships for two years before we earned the right to speak into their lives.

Some supporters think that is a waste of time because the church in the Unites States is not like that. But you cannot build an American church in a foreign country. It destroys their culture. The same rules just do not apply overseas. We have tried very hard not to "American-ize" our churches. They do not worship like Americans. Dennis preaches the gospel. If the Word convicts them on something in their culture, Dennis always tells them it is between them and God. He never preaches against their culture.

If we could have done things differently we would have gone to language school for two years before we came to Panama. The language barrier is very hard and you are not very productive when you cannot communicate. Many supporters think that language school is not needed and they quit supporting a missionary if they are not actively doing something to preach the gospel while they are in language school. I try to explain to them how important it is to be fluent in the language before you start ministering. Most want their missionaries to be holding a Bible study the first six months that they are in language school. Can you imagine if you went to China and had to learn the language and on top of that pressure tried to speak enough Chinese to hold a Bible study? In reality, by that stage, you could give away your only child and not even know what you have said! It is better to get a good handle on the language before you start to minister.

Some pastors might suggest hiring a translator. The problem with that is most missionaries cannot afford a translator. They are just surviving at that point. Translators are expensive. Most charge $100 per event. In our case, it would take us two days to get to our destination and two days to get back. So if we had a three-day crusade we were looking at $700. At that time we were only making $350 a month support and we had four children.

Language school is the hardest thing that I have ever done in my whole life. The divorce rate is very high in language school. Most schools teach you a language with the system of peer pressure. You have maybe five students in your class and they play one against the other to pressure you into learning. I was home-schooling four children, doing all the cleaning and cooking, and trying to learn a language on top of it. Many days I would run out of the room crying because of all the pressure that they put on me. No one spoke one word of English. It is all taught in the new language. You can't imagine how hard it is to learn, and understand, something when you cannot even comprehend the instructions!

I always try to share with the pastors the importance of writing encouraging letters to their missionaries. Just because they moved doesn't mean they no longer need a pastor. More than any other time they need you then. Most home churches never communicate with their missionaries. Some only send a form letter. On holidays they never send a card or anything to make them feel loved by their pastor. It is so hard being away from all of your family on the holidays. Missionaries really need extra encouragement during this time.

We had a pastor that wrote to us every month when we first left for the field. His name was Pastor Greg Roe. We would read his letters over and over again to encourage ourselves. It meant so much that someone loved and cared about us. It was not a form letter that he sent to all his supporting missionaries. I understand why that is done, but nothing touches a missionary's heart like a personal letter especially if their home church pastor writes it. Pastor Greg personally typed a letter out to us each month. He made it so personal and uplifting. It meant the world to us. I would say it is the most important thing that a pastor can do for a new missionary on the field.

I travel a lot to other countries throughout Central and South America now. I have had the privilege of knowing hundreds of missionaries and pastors' wives. My heart goes out to some of the missionaries. They do without and barely get along because they do not have enough money to support their families and minister too. The family does without so they can minister. They make incredible sacrifices to preach the gospel. Some of them just break my heart. I wish so much that I could help them. There has to be a way to get more funding to them.

One family of missionaries that I met lived in Honduras and had an apostolic call on their lives. They had seven children and the grandparents had never seen most of the grandchildren. They never had the finances to go home for Christmas or any other time. They had been on the field for 14 years when I first met them. I was preaching, and when the wife walked in, it was like a knife stabbed me in the stomach. I could hardly remember what I was teaching on. I was so moved by her. Afterwards I was talking to her and could understand why God had moved my heart so much for her. She so desperately needed someone to talk to. I listened to her for hours. We have maintained a relationship by e-mail since then. They have established seven churches, I believe. They are such wonderful people and have such a solid ministry. There are hundreds of them out there all alone that need encouragement.

T. L. Osborn said that discouragement sends more missionaries home than anything else. So I encourage you, pastors, to write encouraging letters to your missionaries, remember their birthdays, and send something special for the holidays. Money is the best thing to send because the taxes in other countries are ridiculous. For example, in Panama they charge you $3 for one cassette!

When your missionaries come home, try to lavish your love and materialistic things on them to prove your love for them. They need your love just as much as they need your financial support. It doesn't need to be an expensive thing. One time a lady took our children to a candy store and gave them an empty bag. She told them to fill it with all the candy they wanted. I think she spent $20. I cannot tell you how much that meant to our children. It spoke volumes to them. They have sacrificed a lot to grow up on the mission field.

Most missionaries that are new on the field never get an opportunity to go to a conference for spiritual refreshing. Normally they put on the conferences that refresh others. There has never been a refreshing conference in the jungle unless we were the people putting on the conference. We have never had the opportunity to get away like that.

Something really nice that you could do for a missionary is to pay for them to go away to a conference to be refreshed before they go back on the field. Most conferences for pastors in the States have nothing to do with the missionary's situation. Ideally it could be a seminar that they could relate to and would help them in their situation. A good conference for them would be one on leadership or people skills.

Remember, when they come home to the States they spend most of their time traveling from church to church and they are the speakers. They give out and give out and give out on the field and when they come home it is the same situation. However, sharing in the churches really helps the missionary in one way because they tell their vision over and over and it gets them fired up again about completing the vision that sent them to the field. Coming home to most missionaries is a lot of work. We live out of a suitcase the entire time we are home, traveling hundreds of miles from one church to another. It is very hard.

BACK TO THE JUNGLE

Now I will get back to this season of our lives!

When we got back to the jungle the rains were so severe that we built a thatch roof around the tent because it leaked so badly. Every night we would get soaked in our sleeping bags and literally slept in water. The next morning we would set everything out in the hot 120-degree sun and dry it all out. This went on for another year. We built another grass hut to live in during the day.

We had met a man named Pastor Bill Troyer when we were in the States. He started an organization called "Helping Hands for Missions." He asked us if he could come and bring a team of carpenters with him to start building our house, so he brought the first team down.

We had been buying a few cement blocks every payday so we had enough to put cement blocks up, three high, all around the house plus pour the cement floor. Every year he would come and continue to build the house with the blocks we were able to purchase.

Pastor Troyer brought another group and put on the roof of the house. Dennis said to me, "Why don't we move into the house? It has a roof to keep us dry." So that is what we did.

Reality hit me when we moved out of the tent into the unfinished house. Talk about God's grace! When we moved into the house, Dennis built us beds of 2x4's and plywood. They were three feet off the ground and we put sleeping bags on them. We draped our mosquito nets over the top of the rafters. The nets were then tucked under our sleeping bags to keep all the insects off of us.

That night I felt so good sleeping in the house for the first time. All the kids had their own rooms separated by a wall of three cement blocks high. For me it was a romantic moment to be treasured. We thanked God for His abundant provision.

Dennis is the type of person that nothing fazes. There is no situation that can get him upset. He loves danger. He thrives on situations in which he could possibly die. You can always count on him to be steadfast and to have a calm head in the worst of situations.

I had to go to the bathroom so I got my flashlight. When I shined it on the floor to get out of bed, the floor was crawling with snakes. I totally freaked out! I woke Dennis up and asked him to go with me to the bathroom.

Dennis had so much patience with me and was always so sweet to comfort my fears. I cried, "Dennis, the floor has snakes all over it!" He calmly replied, "Jeanne, you live in the jungle. There are snakes in the jungle." That was a real revelation to me because I never thought about snakes when we lived in the tent. It had a floor that was zippered all around us and I somehow never thought about it. For two years I never realized the world that came alive every night in the jungle. I began to understand what nocturnal animals were all about!

Then there was the toilet. Dennis's idea of a toilet was a chrome chair with the cushion taken out of it. We just moved it around from place to place. On the way to the chrome toilet we had to pass a large septic tank that had not been covered yet. It had filled up with water. It rains 150 inches of rain over a period of nine months in the jungle. I heard a big splash in the water as we walked around the septic tank.  I asked, "What's that?" Dennis said, "It is an alligator. Jeanne, you live in the jungle and there are alligators in the jungle."

We lived in the unfinished house, without electricity or running water, for twelve years and little by little we added cement blocks to the house. The only child who has lived in the finished house is our youngest son, Chad.

FOOTSTEPS OF FAITH

Every night in the unfinished house, rats and everything you could imagine swarmed the house. Bats flew in, diving from room to room. Their feces are deadly and have been proven to cause cancer.

The snakes were the greatest fear I had to face in that house while it was being built. There is a snake called the 24-hour snake. This snake is not big around but gets pretty long. It climbs in bed with you and hugs the form of your body. When you move, it bites you, and you never wake up. For six years the fear of losing one of our children by a snake bite tormented me. Every night for six years I would go from bed to bed checking on the children, looking for snakes. We found this type of snake twice in our oldest son's bed. I would wake Dennis up and he would come with a machete. He would slide the machete gently between the child's body and the snake. Then, very quickly, he flicked the snake into the air and cut its head off. This snake's head can bite you up to five hours after it has been severed. The nerves keep the snake biting, and if it bites you, it is just as deadly as when it was alive. The head had to be buried immediately so none of our zillions of pets would get near it.

Jonas Gingerich came every year and built the rest of the house. He has built just about everything in our ministry. God is so good. Jonas is an Amish contractor and our home is beautiful. Everything inside is wood and really built in perfection. The Amish are known for their work. I never dreamed I would have a home built by the Amish. Jonas is a good friend and a tremendous blessing in our personal lives.

THE ZOO

Dennis let the kids have all kinds of pets. It was a zoo at our house! They had monkeys, baby tigers, and saino pigs or wild boars. They had it all, except he would not let them have snakes since there were so many poisonous ones.

He bought Jennifer a horse. She absolutely loved horses and always dreamed of having her own. The horse helped her adjust to the jungle. She would hurry up each day and get her schoolwork done, then she was with her horse the rest of the day. She would ride for hours.

Dennis bought Chad a horse also. He named him Pepi. He was not a good horse. Chad needed a hobby and was not into sports very much. Jason was the only one who could handle Chad's horse. All four kids rode the horses almost every night. They rode like they were born to ride.

Jennifer's horse had a baby. She named him Sebastian. He was beautiful. In the morning you could see him running like lightning all over the fields.

Jason loved animals and one time Dennis let him bring home five baby saino pigs. They are basically wild boars. He raised them until they were big and then sold the meat.

Chris and Jason would get exotic birds and non-poisonous boa snakes and sell them to the American military soldiers. They had everything from 16-foot boa snakes to beautiful macaw birds.

Our oldest boy, Chris, had a pet cusumbi. This animal is very loving and tame. It looks like a cross between a raccoon and a possum and eats insects in trees. It would climb trees and stick out its skinny, very long tongue until it was full of insects. Then it very quickly sucked it back into its mouth.

The cusumbi was nocturnal, and even though we made so many cages for it, none of them kept it in at night. This animal loved Dennis. Every night it would crawl into our wooden plank bed and cuddle up with Dennis. It would stick its tongue in Dennis's ear. This, of course, would wake Dennis up, so Dennis convinced Chris to give the animal away.

Chris even had a baby tiger at one time. When the tiger turned 6 months old, we had to turn it lose, though, because it was quick as lightning and had razor-sharp claws. Tigers only eat raw meat. We kept it in a cage. We would try to put meat in the cage before it would get our hands, but it was too quick and really clawed the kids' hands. There is just no way that you can convince me that you can tame a wild tiger cub.

One time when Chris and I were going into the city we saw a black panther run across the road with her cub. She was really beautiful, running so gracefully in front of us. They are beautiful animals but I sure would not want to come upon one alone in the jungle without a gun. They are quick as lightning and incredibly strong. They can drag things that are double their weight for many miles. There is nothing that they cannot overpower.

The kids had talking birds and taught them to say everything under the sun. The monkeys loved to torment the birds. They would get under their cages and try to pull their feet through the mesh cage. The monkeys could get into any lock on any cage or door. They would get inside the birds' cages and poke them in the eyes and put their fingers up their nostrils. Chad taught the birds to growl like a tiger, which the monkeys are terrified of, and the monkeys finally left the birds alone.

The kids also had one monkey whose mother was killed before it was weaned. That monkey was convinced that I was his mother. Every time I would come out of the house he would jump on me and start trying to nurse. He was determined, and he was so strong that the only way that I could get him off of me was to punch him in the face and run back into the house!

One time while we were at church the monkeys got into the house. I kept everything in five-gallon containers to keep the bugs out. The monkeys got into the flour and sugar and threw them all over the house. When I walked in I saw that the monkeys were covered with white flour and sugar from head to toe. I quickly showed them out of the house and began cleaning up their mess.

The monkeys loved to ride the backs of our Labrador dogs. They would get on their back and grab the fat around the dog's neck with one hand and grab the dog's tail with the other hand. They would ride for hours screaming like they were on bronco horses. With monkeys around you did not miss anything by not having a television. They would keep us entertained for hours!

Since Dennis was gone a lot I had to deal with the zoo on my own. My greatest challenge was dealing with the snakes. I was so afraid the children would get bitten and I would not get there in enough time and I'd lose them to a snake bite. This fear tormented me so badly that I never slept during the night. I must have gotten out of bed a hundred times each night checking their beds for snakes, so I was exhausted most of the time. This went on for six years.

GROWING UP

Dennis would let the kids do everything. One time he let Jason go wild boar hunting for two weeks with the Indians. I did not sleep for those two weeks until he was home and I knew he was safe. Dennis slept like a baby. To calm my fears, Dennis told me that Jason was with Indians who were specialists in living in the jungle and no one knew more about the jungle and how to survive than they did. He would say, "Relax. He is safe."

By this time the government had passed a law that gave foreigners the right to own a gun, so Dennis bought the boys a .22 rifle. The way you hunt wild boars (we call them mountain pigs here) was to lay on your stomach on the bare ground until  you spotted one. You have one shot with a .22. You must hit the boar right between the eyes to kill him. Keep in mind this is in the pitch black jungle.

Jason and the Indians killed many pigs and a variety of other animals while they were gone. They slept in hammocks tied to trees, drank out of rivers, and caught all the food they ate. I could just imagine Jason laying on the ground and encountering a black snake, one of the aggressive fast snakes that are attracted to light, looking right into his flashlight! Jason had the time of his life, however, and came home a champion hunter.

The boys loved to hunt on our 68 acres of jungle. Before we were allowed to own guns the boys hunted with machetes. One time they went hunting and came home about sunset after being gone all day. They were acting funny so I began asking them about their day.

Chad has always been the one with the biggest conscience, who will rat on everyone else and tell you what really happened. Jason went on and on about a snake he had killed. Chad interrupted and said, "That's how Pee Wee's tail got chopped off. Jason was swinging at the snake, Pee Wee got in the way, and Jason cut his tail off!" Pee Wee was one of our golden Labs. Bowser was the other one.

I helped them bandage up Pee Wee's tail, and we cauterized it so infection would not set in. There were no vets in the Darien Jungle.

Dennis would buy me a small pig for my birthday each year. I love pigs. We would raise the pig for a year and then kill it and have a big pig roast. One pig we had got so big that he looked like something out of a horror show. He was mean too. A neighbor said that we should castrate the pig. Of course, we did not know any different. So our boys and Dennis and a few neighbors held the pig down. He was fighting mad! One neighbor castrated the pig with a really sharp machete. That pig threw everyone clear across the yard! The neighbor laughed and laughed because we should have done this when the pig was little. That pig was the mildest-mannered pig that you would ever want after that! We learned not to wait until they were so big to castrate them.

We also had a chicken pen and raised chickens for many years. It was Chad's job to gather the eggs each morning. One morning he came running back in and said, "Mom, all the baby chickens are gone and all of the eggs." I said, "It is either a snake or a possum." So that night the boys waited for the animal to appear. Sure enough, it was a possum. He went right for the eggs, and Jason shot him with a gun.

Life was a lot of fun, but it was also very hard. There were no modern conveniences and everything had to be done the hard way.

We lived off of the land so we had a garden. That garden was a nightmare! Everything had to be done by hand. Weeding was a daily chore for all of us. The vegetables would get just about big enough to pick and the monkeys would decide to pick all of the cabbage and tomatoes and throw them at each other. I asked the Indians what to do about it. They told me that monkeys hate owls. So I bought a big plastic owl. Its eyes glowed in the dark. 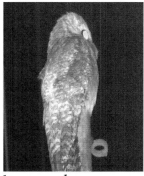 The monkeys would not go near that garden because they were so afraid of the owl!

We did not have any electricity for 12 years. Everything had to be prepared and cooked the day that you ate it. If anything was left over, the dogs or the pigs would get it. Not much was ever left over, though, because the boys were big eaters.

Our normal breakfast was pancakes. Then for lunch we had soup and rice. Every night we ate rice and some kind of bean. Sometimes we would make ripe plantanos to have something sweet. When we killed a chicken or went fishing we had meat. We did not have any red meat in our diet. I did not feel comfortable buying meat from the truck going down the road that sold it. Flies were all over it, and who knew when they killed it!

During those first six years fear tormented me so much that I was exhausted most of the time. Torment takes a toll on your physical body. I was so afraid that we would lose one of the children to a snake bite. Snakes were in everything. In the kitchen everything was in boxes. The snakes would have babies in the boxes, and the small ones are the deadliest. I remember being so scared, and cautious, about putting my hands in the boxes.

Bats flew through the house each night like it was a video game. Every night two of the boys would be on bat patrol. One would have a butterfly net to knock the bat out of the air and the other one would kill it with a machete.

There are many different kinds of bats in the jungle. We had a lot of the vampire bats. They had a numbing agent on their tongues and would lick your toes or fingers and then suck your blood out. Even though bats are a natural mosquito and insect killer, it was better to kill them. The mosquitos here are carriers of the Dengue fever and malaria. The Lord really protected us, though, because none of us were ever bitten.

 We finally built an outhouse with walls around it. The hole was 30 feet deep and was dug by hand. The outhouse had a cement floor in it. We also made a shower in it by putting a 55-gallon drum on top of the roof and piping it into the bathroom. Unfortunately the moisture in the bathroom made it a nesting place for tarantulas and scorpions so you had to be really careful when you went in there. And one night a huge snake, probably 16 feet long, was draped all across the top of the shower. Needless to say, it did not take me long to take a shower!

POWER OVER SNAKES

In one of the churches the pastor was having a problem with a witch who would prophesy in church every meeting. She would say, "Thus saith the Lord, 'The pastor's wife is sleeping with the worship leader.'" The pastor had talked to her several times but she would not take his counsel, so he asked Dennis to visit her. I went with him.

We drove halfway up the mountain road when the jeep hit something that it could not get over. This was very strange because that jeep could get over anything. Dennis said we would walk the rest of the way, so he got out first and jumped over what appeared to be a large tree. It was all the way across the road. When I raised my leg up to step over the "tree," the snake raised its head up. It must have been 16 feet long and huge in diameter. I froze! Dennis came back over the snake and told me it was just a boa snake and it wouldn't hurt me. I knew that boa snakes swallowed small cows whole, but Dennis quickly reminded me that they had to be in trees to fall on their prey and then they would put a numbing agent on the prey, choke it to death, and then swallow it whole. I just could not get my leg to go over that snake for anything so Dennis carried me over it. Of course, all the way up the mountain I was looking to see if there was another one because some snakes run in pairs.

When we got up to the witch's house she asked us how we got up there. Dennis told her we walked. "Didn't you see my snake?" she asked. "I sent him to keep you from coming here." When she said that, something inside of me clicked. I thought, if the devil has power over a snake and it obeys him, then how much more power does a child of God have! Dennis told the witch that she could no longer come to church. The witches and witch doctors were afraid of Dennis so she never came back to church again.

I began taking authority over the snakes in the house when we got home. I would shout the name of Jesus and run like mad. Ha! Eventually I was able to take my authority and stand still and make the snake run. It took me a few years to get it right, but I did!

"I AM SURE IT IS NOTHING..."

At this time we had lived in the jungle on our land for six years. One night something happened that truly was my breaking point. I was still getting up and checking on the kids' beds each night. I had gotten out of bed and when I got back into bed I felt something in my hair. I told Dennis there was something in my hair. He said, "I am sure it is nothing, Jeanne." I said, "No, there is something scratching in my hair." So he got a flashlight and looked in my hair. I always wore it up in a bun on the top of my head at night because it was so hot. It was then that he said, "Oh, Jeanne, you are going to have to be a big girl about this one. When you got out of bed to check the kids' beds there was a rat in the rafters that lost her footing and fell on your pillow. The fall must have caused her to go into labor. When you got back into bed and laid your head on the pillow she must have crawled into your hair and had her babies." I was hysterical! I have no clue whatever happened to those rats. I cried for two weeks straight. I could not get past the rats in my hair. I told the Lord that I did not know that it would be so hard. I was ready to leave the mission field. I had come to the end of my strength and just could not go on anymore.

The Lord told me over my morning coffee to start writing a journal of all the times He had been faithful to us over the years...all the miracles and signs and wonders. By this time I had seen seven people raised from the dead and hundreds of miracles. I began writing, and the Lord healed me of the rat experience by remembering how faithful He had been over the years.

After I quit crying, the Lord told me to put my hand into His. I could feel His hand taking my hand. He told me that from that time on I would always feel His tangible presence with me. He told me I no longer needed to feel alone and that I would know He was with me everywhere I went. To this day I feel His presence with me every day.

That night I was lying in bed and I asked Him to help me to be able to sleep at night. Fear plagued my life so much and tormented me every night. I had the most incredible experience with God. I felt my body fly up and out of the house. I was high above the earth and I was soaring on the wings of an eagle. I flew with the Lord far above my circumstances every night for about one year. I could see everything from a different perspective. I will always be thankful for the time I cried out to Him and He rescued me from all of my fears. I slept like a baby every night and woke up totally refreshed. I never again checked the kids' beds for snakes. Soaring with Him on the eagle's wings healed me and made me realize how very deeply He loved me.

I am a real worshipper of God. Even to this day I can feel my body fly with God when I am in deep worship. I get totally lost, and it seems like hours pass being lost in His presence.

A SHIELD OF PROTECTION

That next month Dennis was gone with his team when two Panamanian pastors came to the house. They asked me to take them to where a man had been bitten by a snake and was dying. So the two pastors, our oldest son, and I jumped into the jeep and off we went. As we were driving along a man flagged me down and asked if I would give him a ride, so I did. When he got into the car I knew that he was a witch doctor. My son squeezed my leg to make sure I knew that he was a witch doctor. I asked the witch doctor where he was going and he said the same place we were going.

When we arrived, the witch doctor quickly got out of the jeep and went into the land where the dying man was. It was about a quarter of a mile from the road. When we got ready to go in, the witch doctor said in a very loud and authoritarian demonic voice, "You are not welcome here." So the two pastors preached the gospel from the road, hoping the man who was dying would accept Jesus into his heart before he died.

A crowd began to gather on the road where the pastors were yelling the gospel. Several people were born again. Then a young man came up to one of the pastors and said, "This man that is dying is my best friend. I will go in there and tell him about Jesus." The pastor told the young man to lay hands on the dying man and command that he be healed. Of course, the young man knew nothing about his authority in the name of Jesus, but he did what the pastor told him. The dying man jumped up off of his deathbed totally healed! The witch doctor was so angry.

I went down the lane, thinking that they would let us in now. I was caught up in the spirit realm. It was as if a bubble engulfed my whole body. The bubble was a very hard shield that nothing could get through. At that time I saw missiles flying through the air. They were death missiles sent to kill me. When they hit the shield, they would go back on the witch doctor and hit him and he would scream. This happened about three times and each time the witch doctor got angrier.

Then the Lord told me that there was a shield around me that no witch doctor or devil could penetrate to get to me.

> *He shall cover thee with his feathers, and under his wings*
> *shalt thou trust: his truth shall be thy shield and buckler.*

PSALM 91:4

From that day on I was never afraid of witch doctors. I could stand in the middle of some really wild demonic manifestations and never be afraid. Once a witch doctor turned into the form of a crow and landed on a fence post near me. The Indians immediately froze in their steps. When I asked them what was wrong they told me that the crow was the witch doctor. I was not afraid of him at all. He flew away and turned back into his normal body. I don't know how they do that, but I do know it is not of God!

THE NAME OF JESUS

Then there was the time that I woke up in the night and saw a beautiful large figure that looked like an angel. I was in awe at the beauty and the Lord spoke to me, "Even the devil can come as an angel of light, but do not be deceived." At that moment the angel turned into a huge black angel. He said with a very deep evil voice, "I have come for your soul tonight." I was so scared I could not move. Finally, I screamed out the name of Jesus. The black angel instantly disappeared

FOOTSTEPS OF FAITH

and never came back.

Whenever the witches would make medicine against us, I would hear them chanting in the night. I could see their faces in the supernatural realm. I knew who they were. I would speak to them and tell them that it is written that no evil shall befall us and the Lord has given His angels charge over us to keep us safe all the day and all of the night (Psalm 91:10-11, Luke 4:10). The chanting would stop. Many times I would be in the villages the next day and see one of the witches who tried to harm us in the night. When I would look into her dark evil eyes it was like lightning would go out of my eyes into hers and she would run away from me. The witches would check me out a lot when we would go into villages. I never backed down. I would look at them right in their eyes and they would see the power that lived inside of me and they would always back down (1 John 4:4). They knew that greater was He that lived in me than he that lived in the world.

It got to be a funny thing when we would go into a village. Everyone who was not walking with God would come to us and confess their sin. They were sure that we knew they were not walking with God! Until this day I can be in a village and if someone is not saved, my heart cries inside for their soul.

As Dennis traveled from village to village holding Bible schools, a witch doctor would follow him. He would arrive before Dennis in every village. Dennis asked him if he knew a short cut. He smiled and said, "I do not travel like you do. I travel in the air. I am translated from one place to another. I can come and go when I want."

One time an Indian came to our house in the middle of the night and asked Dennis to come to the village of Los Monos with him. When they got there a witch doctor from an island called Moggi (three days by canoe) had just come walking over the river water and was appearing in each young girl's house who was pregnant with her first baby. The witch doctor was telling them that if they accepted Jesus as their Lord and Savior they would all lose their first baby. A witch doctor's greatest power is found within the spirit of fear. One girl got so scared that she aborted her baby.

Then he went house to house visiting each member of the church. Dennis gathered them all together and began reminding them of the authority that they had in the name of Jesus. The witch doctor appeared where Dennis was and said, "I will burn this church to the ground!" Dennis dared him to try. The witch doctor left. The Indians begged Dennis to spend the night with them. Dennis told them it would be

114

better for them if they learned to stand up to the devil on their own, and he would come back the next day to check on them. The witch doctor did not return that night.

The next day Dennis began teaching a series on the authority of the name of Jesus. If I remember right, he taught for six weeks straight. Because the people stood strong on the name of Jesus, the witch doctor never returned to their village.

ELIZABETH

There was a time in the Indian culture if a young woman got pregnant before wedlock she would be cast into the jungle and no one was allowed to help her or even talk to her. She survived alone for nine months. Then she had to deliver her own baby. For the sake of the baby she would be allowed back into the village once the baby was born. I have only known one girl to be shunned like that in all our years of living in the jungle.

A young woman came to our house in the middle of the night. This young girl was being shunned by her village. She said that she drank rat poison to abort her baby. She was five months pregnant, if I remember right. The baby was born and was alive. She brought it to me and told me she didn't want the baby and then left. I had never seen a baby so little.  I weighed her; she weighed one and a half pounds.

The Lord told me to strap the baby to my chest and not to unstrap her. He told me that the life of God inside of me would keep the baby alive. He also told me that this was the best incubator. So I did it. She was so little and helpless that I wanted to cry. It was not fair that someone would take her out of the womb so young. I got the liquid out of her lungs and she was breathing fine. She was not developed enough to be able to suck so I had to feed her with an eye dropper.

I knew the father of the baby, so the next day I went to the village and talked to the chief. He asked us to keep the baby and see if we could get her medical attention. I took her to Panama City the next day with her father to register the birth. The baby died twice on the way to town. Her father prayed for her and God brought the baby back to life. The doctor who saw her said to me, "Why don't you let this child die? She will never live and, if she does, she will be a vegetable." I insisted that he give her a physical examination. He did the exam and came back and said, "She is so retarded that she cannot even suckle. She will not be anything but a vegetable. She will never sit up on her own and she will never walk and play with the children in her village. Let her die in peace." I told him that this child would not die!

When she was 3 months old and weighed 5 pounds I was bringing her back to the same doctor and she died in the car. She quit breathing. I lifted her up out of the car seat and began crying out to God. She had no vital signs. As I was praying over this small baby she began breathing again. When I arrived at the doctor's office the doctor became very angry when he saw me. He said, "I told you the child is not worth saving." I asked him if she could begin her baby shots, but he told me she did not weigh enough to begin her shots. So I left and when the baby was 8 months old I brought her back to the same doctor. When I saw him, he said, "I told you not to bring that baby back here." When he looked at the baby, however, he said, "Oh, I see this is not the same child." He gave her a physical and asked me how old the baby was. I told him she was 8 months old. He asked me if this was the baby I brought to him before and I said, "Yes!" "I have never seen anything like this," he said. "This child is totally normal!" He gave her the first series of her baby shots.

While we were caring for the child she died three times. Once she was with her father and died on the way to town. At that time it took 10 hours to get to town. He was in a bus and was on his way to the doctor. When he took the baby in to see the doctor, the doctor said, "I am sorry that you have come so far, but your child is dead and has been dead for a few hours." The baby's father asked if he could see her. He went in and prayed for the baby and the baby came back to life. The doctor had never seen anyone raised from the dead and did not know what to do with it! The baby's father shared with him about God and left with his baby.

The grandmother wanted the child. Dennis made me promise that we would never adopt a child in the jungle. He knew we would  have 50 million because I would want to rescue everyone in a bad situation! I gave the baby, who I named Elizabeth, back to her grandmother.

One day, four years later, I was in a village and the Indians had a surprise for me. We were in church and in ran this little 4-year-old child. She jumped into my arms and called me mommy. There was no way that child remembered me. What a special gift God gave to me that night!

When Elizabeth turned 5, her grandmother brought her back to the village of Arraemae where I visited on a regular basis. Her teacher told me that she was one of the smartest children she had ever known. We secretly paid for Elizabeth's schooling each year as she grew up.

The grandmother was a witch and would not let the child be raised in church. Elizabeth did not know the story about how she was my little baby for so long. Every time I saw her there was such a bond between us. She could not understand it and would ask her grandmother, "Who is that lady? For some reason I love her. Is she my mommy?" Her grandmother did not tell her the story. She was told that her father had died and her mother was married to another man.

When Elizabeth got to be a teenager she came to church with some friends of hers. She gave her heart to the Lord one day. She started coming to church off and on. One time we were having a special youth conference.  Every year Mrs. Jackie Long would come to the Darien Jungle and hold special conferences. Elizabeth came to one of the conferences and was baptized by the Holy Ghost. They had a foot-washing service during that conference. I went to wash her feet and she began to cry. I held her in my arms and she asked, "Who are you?" I told her the story of how she was strapped to my chest for eight months. I did not tell her that her mother had drank rat poison and had aborted her at five months. I just told her that it was a very special time in my life when I held her so close to my heart for eight months. She cried and cried and hung in my arms for the longest time.

She is now married and has two babies of her own.

INNOCENCE LOST

The Indians do not have the custom of shunning unwed pregnant girls anymore.

A logging company came into the jungle to cut trees down and export the lumber. Panama has a wide selection of very beautiful wood. When the loggers came in, they went to each of the villages and asked for the 12- to 15-year-old girls to come and work in the wood camps. The fathers consented to let their girls go. Nine months later all the young girls were pregnant. Obviously, there were too many young pregnant girls to be shunned. Every family was affected by this logging company. The loggers were very good to the Indian girls and bought them all kinds of gifts and materialistic things. When the babies were born the loggers took care of the children until their logging company pulled out of the area.

Unfortunately this started a desire for materialistic things and the girls started prostituting in order to get money. It is very common now for young girls to get pregnant outside of wedlock.

There is a small town in the Darien Jungle named Metiti. This town has the only high school in this area. The teens either travel back and forth to their homes or they board in Metiti. There is no supervision of the teens if they board there. The transportation is $3 per day. Most of the teens find a place to live and board there.

We were told by the clinic in that area that this small town had 75 abortions one year; 50 were by Indian girls. The clinic asked us a few years ago to go into the villages and teach on venereal disease. Metiti has the highest rate of AIDS in all of Panama.

When we had trouble with the Colombia anti-military groups coming over the borders of Colombia and into Panama, the police force was doubled. Every fifteen days they change the recruits. The police station is huge and they police the area from Metiti to the Colombian border. This is the cause of the large amount of AIDS. The young police sleep with the young girls in the high school.

Used to be that the Indians never divorced. If they did, their custom was that the woman would take the man's underwear out in the front yard and burn them. Then the marriage was over. Divorce is very common today. Most teens do not get married anymore and sexual disease is beginning to be seen more in the villages.

It has been very sad for us to watch "progress" take a toll on the people here. They used to be so innocent and pure. The jungle has changed so much since we first moved here.

EIGHT YEARS AND COUNTING

By this time we had lived in the jungle for eight years. The house was partially built. The cement walls were finished to the ceiling. There were only holes cut out for the windows and doors. We blocked the holes for the doors with a piece of wood.

I home-schooled the children on the Accelerated Christian Education curriculum. We received the schooling all the way through high school free from Pastor Steve Eckerd.

A friend of ours was a talk show host on a local television show in our hometown. He made a comment about something and I told him that I did not believe that. So we made a bet, who was right or who was wrong. I was sure that I was right, but if I lost I had to go on his talk show. Well, I lost! The host of the program asked our children all kinds of questions. It reminded me of the Bill Cosby show, "Kids Say the Darndest Things."

Their conversation went something like...

"Jason, do you like your teacher?" He knew we home-schooled.

"I hate my teacher." Meaning me.

"Isn't your mom your teacher?"

"Yes!"

"Why do you hate her?"

"She makes me do all my math and she checks all of my work every day."

"What did you think when you moved to the jungle?"

"I thought we were going camping, but we never came home!"

We continued home-schooling. I kept all of the kids' records. A good friend of ours was a principal of a Christian school. I would send him their test papers and he would issue a diploma each year.

Jennifer and Chris graduated from high school. Jennifer was 17 and Chris was 18 years old.

We did not have one dime to send them to college. That summer I took them to the United States to see if I could get them registered into a college. I still did not know how we were going to pay for them to go to college, but we made the trip by faith.

When I took them to the college I showed the admissions counselor their diplomas. The admissions counselor asked, "You home-schooled your children?" When I told her I had, she said, "We are giving the SAT entrance exam tomorrow, but I do not think your kids are prepared to take it." I told her that I would pay for the test ($60 per child) anyway.

The kids took the test the next day. The counselor called me that night and apologized to me. She said, "Mrs. Cook, I am so sorry for being so rude to you about your children taking the SAT exam. You obviously took home-schooling seriously and did an excellent job at educating your children. I am proud to tell you that they both are eligible to receive a full Pell grant which will pay for a five-year degree!" They were even given a housing allowance each month. God provided! Jennifer attended University of Indiana State and Chris went to Purdue State. They are community colleges in the same small town.

Chris has always been really smart. He picked up Spanish so quickly that it was amazing. Dennis used him as an interpreter for years until he learned the language himself. Chris is a born leader and we always knew that he would be very successful in life in whatever field he chose to go into. He always gave 150% to everything that he did and still does today.

Chris married Debra Raber when they graduated from college.

 Chris has an EET (Electrical Engineer Technician degree). They have three children: Nathan, Liliana and Casey.

Jennifer married Rick Fisher when they  graduated from college. He also has an EET degree. They have two children: Joshua and Zachary.

ESTABLISHING MORE NEW CHURCHES

Back in the Darien, Dennis began establishing another church in the village of Meyasito. This village was a long way away. You had to travel three hours by jeep and then another two hours by canoe. The people there were very primitive and knew nothing about God. Dennis loves situations like this when he can begin at the beginning and establish their faith in the foundations of the Bible. He did not build them a physical church. Years later that group of believers merged with another church. We gave our blessing on the merge.

Dennis was gone a lot but it was easier since Jason was 16 and Chad was 15. They were teens, but in many ways they carried the weight of an adult. Dennis had taught them to do almost everything, from building churches to keeping books to fixing broken-down vehicles. They were a big help and did everything that I needed around the house.

We never put the burden on our children that they had to preach the gospel or be in the ministry just because we were. I asked the Lord when the children were small what their gifting was. He showed me the strong areas in each child, and we tried to raise them by encouraging them in those giftings. They are all so different.

Jason is an excellent carpenter and helped his dad build several churches. When Jason turned 17, he went to live with Chris in the States and went to trade school. He married Becky Tucker and they had three children: Brittany, Kristen and Abbi Gaile. The marriage did not work out and they divorced. He then married Lucia Leung and they are very happy. They moved to Panama and  are helping us in the ministry. Pictured are great-grandbaby Caitlyn, mom Brittany, Abbi Gaile, Jason, Kristen, and Jason's wife Lucia.

Chad, our youngest son, is the administrator of the radio station and not married.

Dennis established another church in Pueblo Nuevo, which was closer to our home.

FOOTSTEPS OF FAITH

This church was our greatest challenge. The people were deep into witchcraft and the chief of the village was the witch doctor.

We built a church in that village but had to take it down because Dennis has strict conditions when he builds a church. They cannot use the church building for anything worldly.

The witch doctor began having drinking parties in the church. Dennis told him if he did it again that he would take the church down. Sure enough he had another festival full of drugs, alcohol, and witchcraft, so Dennis came in and took the church down.

Several ministers have tried to raise up a church in that village but never could get the people to sell out 100% to God. The ones who were strong Christians moved from that village over into a village where the chief was a Christian. It amazes me how you can give the opportunity of a lifetime to people and yet they throw it away.

This season of our life had now ended.

CHAPTER FIVE
LIVING ON MIRACLE GROUND

I t seems like everything in our life changed when Chad, our youngest son, went back to the United States to go to college. I had a real identity crisis. It left a great void in my life when our last child left home. I was the administrator of the ministry, and I normally loved my job, but I lost all desire to do anything. I didn't even want to go to church and that is pretty bad when you're the pastor's wife!

Soon afterwards we left for the States to itinerate. As we were visiting the churches, it seemed like wherever we went the pastor's wife would tell me everything going on in her life. I was used to that in the jungle, but I would pray and leave the burden with the Lord. This time it was different. I could not get rid of the burden for pastors' wives. Every time that I would pray about it, God would say, "Change is coming." I was glad because I so desperately needed something to change.

ME? ORGANIZE A CONFERENCE?

One time when I was praying the Lord said to me, "Jeanne, would you do something for Me?" Of course I said yes, but then I almost choked when He told me what He wanted. He asked me to start going into Panama City once a month to organize a conference for pastors' wives. I quickly reminded Him that I was a jungle girl now and that would be a major thing for me. I would have to dress like a girl and wear nylon hose and...you know, do the girl thing. I was not in my comfort zone in that world!

But I began going into the city and I found a lady to organize it for me. I met with her once a month and told her everything that I wanted. The first conference was beautifully organized and it went really well, but I felt grieved inside, like something was wrong. So I asked the Lord what was wrong. He told me He had asked me to organize it, not to delegate it to someone else. For me it was normal to delegate things to other people.

During that conference seven women came up to me and told me they would like to help me with the conference next year. So I formed a staff with those seven women. It is funny how the Lord works. Only a couple of them were Panamanians. One was Costa Rican, one Guatemalan, one from Mexico, and one from Puerto Rico. Every one of the ladies moved to Panama because of job changes or they were sent as missionaries to Panama. It seemed like God moved all of these ladies here to Panama for a time like this. You remember how God put Esther from the Old Testament in a place when He wanted something done?

We began planning the conference for the next year. I didn't know many people in Panama City, but my staff knew everyone. The talent of that group of ladies was amazing. For everything that I needed done, one of them seemed to have a degree in that very thing!

Together we planned a conference that would change all of our lives forever. The Lord always gave me the lessons for the conference in worship. He gave me every little detail that He wanted to cover in each class. I asked Him why He was so detailed. For me, that is a funny question because I am such a detail person. He said each of the details was birthed out of a pastor's wife crying out in the night to Him. He wanted to make sure everything was answered for them.

I put the announcement for the conference out over the radio station in Panama City.

Sixty-eight pastors' wives from 19 different denominations attended the second conference. It was the first pastors' wives conference that went across all denominations in Panama and many of the surrounding countries. In the natural you would not think anyone would attend because each denomination had their own conferences, but these conferences changed the way all of the denominations ministered to their pastors and their wives.

Each woman that came said when they heard the announcement over the radio the Lord called them by name and told them He had a divine appointment set up for them at the conference. Boy, you couldn't get any better advertisement than that!

I chose my team of seasoned teachers very carefully. I wanted them to be in the ministry for at least ten years serving as a pastor's wife. I had to make sure that they were the ones God chose to lead a conference that would change the lives of pastors' wives forever. They had to have a heart toward uniting denominations. They also had to have a heart for pastors' wives.

Team members were Rallene Almendarez, Jeaneen Klahr, Teri Roe, Terri Porter, Ann Windsor, and Carol Fitch, left to right, in the picture to the right.

The lady that I asked to lead worship was on my staff. Her name was Vyana Pereda. I had heard her sing at a church and the Lord told me to invite her to lead the worship in all of the conferences. I noticed that He said "conferences"... plural.

I asked Vyana (on the left with Rene Mendosa, right) and she accepted. She was thrilled but at the same time intimidated because of the people who would be attending. I guess she didn't feel adequate. She told me she had attended the first conference. Sitting on the front row she said to herself, "I am supposed to be the one leading worship."

That year when she got into the pulpit, an incredible thing happened to her. It was as if she stepped into an anointing unlike anything that she had ever experienced. Years ago someone prophesied over her that she would lead nations into the face of God. She never really thought too much about it until that morning. The anointing that was on her brought every denomination directly into the Holy of Holies. A lot of the denominations had never been in worship before, but they entered right in. It was the most awesome

thing to be a part of. The power of God hit that conference in a way that none of us had ever experienced before.

There were 15 tables of ladies. I wanted to mix them up but they all seemed to gravitate to the people of their denomination. So, we had a Baptist table, an Episcopalian table, an Assembly of God table, and on and on.

The power of God hit so hard that it knocked me 10 feet out of my chair. One of the teachers at my table was thrown up on the wall. She stayed in that position for 45 minutes.

God changed the anointing at every table. People who did not believe in healing were instantly healed. A lady who had an incurable lung disease was instantly healed. Another lady with cancer and on her deathbed was instantly healed.

People who did not believe in the baptism of the Holy Ghost were lifted up off of their feet with their hands extended in the air worshipping God and speaking in other tongues.

There were people from seven nations there and nineteen different denominations.

Two ladies there were from Nicaragua. They came to visit a lady in Costa Rica and she brought them with her to the conference. Their husbands were the heads of a very large denominational church. God spoke to them individually and told them that they had one year to get man's laws out of their churches. They were so shook up that they looked like they had seen a ghost. Later I found out when they went home and shared with their husbands, they fell out in the Holy Ghost and God spoke the same Word to their husbands. It changed that entire denomination!

Another year the Lord was dealing with hurts between the senior pastor's wife and the ones under them. The Lord told me to have the senior pastor's wife wash the feet of a pastor's wife under them.

I called the senior pastor's wife from the largest church in Panama up to begin the foot-washing process. She brought a young missionary from Haiti to the conference. The young lady missionary had been in bed for a year. A curse had been put on her and she was dying. The doctors said she would not live much longer. When the senior pastor's wife put her hands in the water to wash her feet, the girl looked like she had been hit by lightning. She jumped and began to run all over the conference room! The water was so anointed that it broke all of the walls down between them. Pastors' wives across denominations were hugging each other and asking forgiveness for misunderstandings they had with each other.

The senior pastor's wife ran out the door. She returned the next day and shared with me what happened to her. Her best friend had betrayed her in the ministry 10 years ago and she told the Lord that she would never hug or pray for anyone again. She told me that she had been coming to the conferences for five years and each year God healed her a little bit more. It was so hard for her to trust anyone as a friend again. When she put her hands in the water at this conference it was the first time in 10 years she had prayed for anyone. She said the power of God completely healed her heart as well as the young missionary. Today she is totally free from that hurt and prays for people and genuinely loves them like she once did.

When the conference in Panama was five years old I began taking the conferences to different countries in South and Central America.

I had many teachers over the years that traveled with me but my core group was Jody Baker, Joy Hirschy, Rallene Almendarez, and Teri Roe. We taught the same lessons in each country, but the Holy Ghost changed the emphasis for each country.

In Costa Rica it was always a message of getting stronger, being grounded in the Word, and the character of God.

In Colombia His words were always about Him as a God of refuge.

In Nicaragua the message was always on judgment.

The message to Guatemala was always on self-worth.

Panama's message was always on emotional healing.

In Honduras we only had one conference and it was on deception.

For El Salvador the message was about choosing to be free.

Brazil was exhorted to quit fighting and unite denominations.

I could not begin to tell you all of the miracles that took place during those conferences. It was like you stepped into another world and were caught up in the glory cloud for four days.

It was very common in all of the conferences for ladies to remain seated, basking in the presence of God. They did not want to leave that atmosphere. I learned so much while organizing the conferences.

FOOTSTEPS OF FAITH

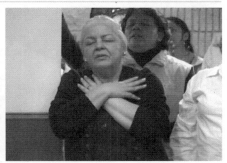

When they were over I felt like I had given birth! It felt so good knowing that I did it God's way.

God was certainly right when He said change was coming to my life. It is amazing what God will do in your life when you agree to make changes. This season was sure a blessing to me.

One of the countries we went into had many denominational churches. Most had never felt the presence of God or been exposed to worship.

The ladies sat there caught up in the presence of God. One lady told me that she had never been in the presence of God before. She said she was afraid, but it caused a hunger inside of her for more of God. Before, she was critical of Spirit-filled people and did not believe in the Holy Ghost.

A lot of the women hit their knees and continued kneeling for what seemed like hours.

One lady crawled to the altar crying hysterically. We found out later that her church and the whole congregation were buried in a mudslide after an earthquake. Ten thousand people were swept under the ground when the earth opened up and swallowed the whole town. She lost her husband and all of their children, everything. She knew she had to get to the conference because she needed to get into the presence of God in order to be able to let the pain out.

Another year we were in Colombia. The pastors' wives had gone through a really hard season and were devastated. They had lost the vision of the call of God on their lives. A young teenager began to play the drums. He played for about an hour and a half. Someone prophesied

that it was a cry for the lost coming through the drums. They were calling to the weary and heavy-laden. The ladies crawled to the altar and when the drums quit they were totally focused on the call of God on their lives. The power was so strong that when the teachers began to
teach there was one spot in the room where they would fall out in the Holy Ghost if they got too near it.

Another time the glory cloud fell and for four days there was a light that shone in the conference. The light seemed to be a supernatural presence of God. No one wanted to leave the conference. They would sit there after the conference just basking in the presence of God. I remember when we teachers went back to our rooms we all just wanted to be alone with God. I cannot tell you what happened in that time we were all caught up in the presence of God because it was different for every woman. For me, it drew me into a deeper walk with Him, a deeper level in the supernatural realm.

There was one time when the Spirit of the Lord fell and we all cried in the conference. No one could quit crying. We must have cried for more than an hour. I cried the rest of the evening. I was so full of stress. Dennis had some health problems the year before and I just about lost him. He had a blood clot pass through his lungs and heart. I was so upset, but trying to be strong, I had not even cried about it. I was able to release all of the stress when I was crying. God totally restored me.

FARC

Many times at the conferences the pastors' wives were so wounded and hurt because of things that they had experienced. This was the case at one of the conferences we held in Colombia.

In Colombia there is a lot of unrest. I live 40 miles from the border of Panama and Colombia. They have two groups of militants plus the drug world. One of the militant groups calls themselves the Fuerzas

Armadas Revolucionarias de Colombia (FARC). They are reported to have 10,000 soldiers, all cold-blooded murderers. They cross over into Panama on a regular basis. They rape and kill for no reason. Life has no value to them.

One time in one of the villages the FARC had come in and cut off the limbs of the children. They put the children in the town square, no one was allowed to go near them, and they bled to death. What do you say to someone who has seen such evil?

Most of that conference was spent with ladies crying all through the meeting. This kind of crying came from deep inside. I could hardly handle it. Only God could heal such broken hearts.

One lady shared that in their hometown of Cali there was a young missionary couple who started a church. The church grew and grew. Cali was one of the safe zones for the FARC.

The head of FARC decided that he did not like the difference this church had made, so he sent one of his assassins to kill them. Every group has its own way of murdering. This group would kill people by driving by on a motorcycle and shooting them with an automatic weapon.

The people in Cali walked to church every night. When the young man on the cycle from FARC came down the street, he aimed his gun towards them but then dropped his gun and sped off. When the head of FARC heard of the incident he sent him a message: "You know too much and if you do not get your stuff together we will send another person to kill you and the missionary couple who started the church." The young man walked around like he was in a daze.

So the head of FARC sent two men to kill him and the young couple. They pointed their guns to kill the young couple and the same thing happened to them...they dropped their guns and sped off. They found the young man who they were sent to kill but could not kill him either. All three of them were walking down the street and a complete stranger came up to them and said, "Jesus loves you." They fell on the ground and accepted Jesus into their lives.

That night they went to the young couple's church. The three men stood up and one of them gave this testimony. He said that when he was 10 years old his father gave him his first automatic weapon. His father was one of the best assassins in the FARC. They went into a village and his father said to him, "This is the day that you become a man. Your assignment is to kill all the women and children in the village." He murdered them all.

All he ever knew was hatred and murder. When he went to kill that young missionary couple he said there was a force around them that caught him off guard. So much love emanated from them that he felt alive and had so many feelings that he had never felt before. He had no defense against it. He had never felt love before. It left him totally defenseless. All he knew was that he wanted what they had. He could no longer murder people with this love that he craved. He is a pastor today inside the FARC camp and many of them are getting born again!

When I heard this story it made me realize that there is no one so hard-hearted that God doesn't know how to reach them.

A LOVE SONG FROM GOD

We were in El Salvador one year and the ladies in the conference were so hard. It was like they were not able to open up and let God move. There was a young girl with a guitar who led us in worship. God used her in a mighty way to break down the barriers of the women's hearts.

She sang supernaturally the love song that God used to draw her heart to Him. It was a song from the Spirit of God. She played a melody, and the girls that sang with her sang the back-up to the song even though they had never heard it before. They were caught up in the supernatural realm as God used them to minister to the ladies.

The Lord gave me a story and during that story it was like a supernatural drawing of the ladies. We were all caught up in the story. God healed so many of the ladies as they heard the voice of Jesus sing a love song to them.

The story was about a young girl.

THE LITTLE BALLERINA
By Jeanne Cook

Once upon a time in a far away land lived a young king. He was the most powerful king in the entire kingdom. It was a custom in that land that when a young girl turned 14 years old the king would send a carriage for her. You could hear the carriage coming for miles and miles as the roads were cobblestone. As the king's carriage would get closer to the young

girl's home the excitement in her heart would be overwhelming.

The young girls would be taken to the king's palace for a period of two years. There they would bathe all the young girls in the finest perfume and oils. They would brush their hair daily and put all kinds of ointment on it to make it shine like the moonlight.

They would teach the young girls how to talk at the royal table and in all formal meetings. They learned everything necessary to become a beautiful princess.

The young girls were given ballerina lessons so they would learn to move gracefully and be able to dance like they were flowing in the wind. This was very important because they could be asked to dance before the king if he called their name.

On this bright sunny day you could hear the king's carriage coming for miles and miles. But the little girl that the carriage was coming for was not listening. She had forgotten that it was her birthday. You see, her life was nothing to celebrate. They did not even give her a name at birth. They only called her "Little Girl."

She did not know who her mother or father was and she did not have any brothers or sisters. Abandoned at birth, her life was filled with suffering and poverty. She never went to school like all the other little girls, but stayed at home and worked in her shabby little worn-out shack. She had no sweet memories of special times or a loving family. She was abused in every way possible and was used by everyone in the house. She merely existed from one day to another.

When the king's carriage came to her door, it arrived unnoticed. She heard a knock on the door. It was an unusual knock. The man at the door called out to her, "Little Girl, the king has requested your presence in his palace."

She looked out through the dirty glass windowpane. Her eyes filled with amazement and despair and her thoughts went a mile a minute. What would the king want with a life as horrible as mine? What could he possibly want from me? Doesn't he know I am nothing and have nothing that I could offer him? Why would he even bother to send his carriage for me? Doesn't he know what a horrible life I have had?

The voice outside the door kept insisting that she come with him to the palace.

The young girl opened the door. "Is your name Little Girl?," he asked. She answered, "That is what they call me." He said, "The king has requested your presence in the palace."

The chauffeur opened the door to the royal carriage. She felt so unworthy to walk up the fine polished steps into the carriage. She was dirty and ugly and unkempt, but she crawled into the carriage and sat on the fine leather seats. She had never seen anything so beautiful. The carriage was far greater than anything she had ever seen or been in. She began to tremble with fear as her eyes filled up with tears. Why would he send his carriage for me? Doesn't he know who I am and what a horrible life I have lived?

The carriage stopped at the royal palace. The chauffeur reached out his hand for the little girl as he helped her out of the carriage. She was brought into a very large room where hundreds of other little girls, all 14 years old, were present. All of them, like herself, would begin their training on their 14th birthday.

At the end of their two years of beautification they would be invited to a royal banquet. At this royal banquet only one little girl's name would be called out. That little girl would rise up on her feet and dance before the king. If he was pleased with her, then she would be asked to live in the palace, as part of the royal family, and become a princess for the rest of her life. Then one day the king would gather all the princesses together and choose a bride for himself.

As she began her training, all the other little girls were so overjoyed about being there. They laughed and giggled until all hours of the night. This little girl cried herself to sleep every night. She felt so unworthy to be in the palace, let alone be trained to dance before the king. She went through all of the training, but her heart just was not in it.

Every day they would take ballerina lessons for two hours. The class was held in a room full of mirrors. As the little girls danced before the mirrors they began to see themselves as princesses, except this one little girl. She was clumsy and could not dance like the other girls. She avoided the mirrors because she did not want to see herself.

Finally the big day came. They all had a hard time sleeping the night before in anticipation that their names would be called. All but this one particular little girl who did not want her name called. She did not even have a name. The girls called her Esmeralda, but that was just the name the other girls gave to her. She really did not even feel worthy of having a name.

Preparations were being made in the palace for the big banquet to take place. The fresh flowers could be smelled all over the palace. Everything was so beautiful.

FOOTSTEPS OF FAITH

On the day of the great banquet the little girls danced into the king's ballroom. All the little girls, now 16 years old, were dressed in pale pink ballerina costumes. They gracefully sat on the floor in a line seven deep, as they had practiced for the past two years, that draped around the king's throne. As the music stopped, the great moment of anticipation was upon them. The trumpet was blown and a name was called.

The name "Little Girl" was the name the king had chosen! She was paralyzed with fear and could not rise up to dance. She began to cry. There was such a long time between the time that name was called and when the king got up from his throne. He searched everywhere for the little girl. Her teacher nudged her and told her, "Get up, Little Girl. Dance before the king." She said, "I can't get up."

Then the king's eyes, searching throughout the whole room, found the little girl. She looked directly into his loving eyes. He began to sing a love song to her, as their eyes were bonded together. At first when she got up to dance she fell down. She kept looking into the king's eyes and concentrating on the song he was singing. His words made her feel so beautiful.

(Following is the song that the young lady sang to the women at the conference. The words of the song kept repeating.)

"My love surrounds you, healing all the unlovely in your heart.
Until there will be no memory of anything but loveliness.
We will live forever lost in the love of my heart.
For you are the fairest of 10,000 princesses.
Your eyes shine like the morning sun.
Your skin, so soft and beautiful. It glistens in the moonlight.
You flow like an angel as you dance before me.
Forever I will love you. Forever I will caress you.
Forever I will protect you.
For my love will surround you and heal all the unlovely in your
   heart.
Until there will be no memory of anything but loveliness.
We will live forever lost in the love of my heart."

Looking into his eyes she felt the love she had yearned for all of her life. She got back up and tried to dance again. She began to dance and dance and dance. The little girl began twirling around and around *and around until all her life unraveled before her. She could feel that his love covered all the bad things that had ever happened to her.*

In his eyes she had no past. All she had was the present. She began to leap into the air when she realized that she was free from all her past. She danced for hours before the king as he sang the sweetest melody she had ever heard.

Then out of complete exhaustion she fell at the feet of her king. He reached down with his hand and gently took her hand into his, raising her to her feet. She was trembling with fear. He took her into his arms and gently held her there. He hugged her for so long that time seemed to stand still.

Then she began to cry uncontrollably in his arms. He lifted her head and began to push her hair away from her tear-covered face. He held her lovely face in his hands as he admired her beauty. He kissed her tenderly and said, "Of all the princesses in the land, you are the fairest of them all. Would you do me the great honor of sitting at my right side and becoming my queen for eternity?"

The little girl began to smile and out of her heart these words began to flow: "All my life I have heard about your great love. When you sent your carriage for me, I was so scared. But then I remembered the stories of your immense love. It calmed my fears. When you called my name your words seemed to explode with life, with hope, and love. As I heard your heart sing the most beautiful melody I had ever heard, I began to desire to be with you. Everything within me wanted to run to you. The harder I danced, the freer I became, until all my fears had vanished before my eyes.

"As you looked into my eyes I saw your unconditional love for me. No one had ever loved me before. I saw the pureness of your heart. As you embraced me I felt safe from all of my fears. I knew that I could trust you to take care of me, to be a refuge for me, a strong tower in time of need."

The king gently dropped her hand and began to dance. He danced all over the banquet hall with endless energy. The little girl began to smile as he danced around her, time and time again with such overwhelming joy. He then took the little girl's hand in his and whispered into her ear, "May I have this dance with you?" The little girl began to cry as she sweetly answered, "For the rest of my life."

As he took her into his arms they began to dance all over his vast kingdom. They danced all over the streets of gold. From star to star they waltzed all over the universe, riding on the clouds and jumping

---

over the moon in each other's arms. Then they made their way back to the banquet hall.

As he began to show her the mansion that he had spent his life preparing for her, the little girl began to cry as she gently whispered into his ear, "Thank you for saving me. Thank you for choosing me. Thank you for loving me. Thank you for waiting for me."

He smiled and sang this song to her:

*"My love surrounds you, healing all the unlovely in your heart.
Until there will be no more memory of anything but loveliness.
We will live forever lost in the love in my heart.
For you are the fairest of 10,000 princesses.
Your eyes shine like the morning sun.
Your skin, so soft and beautiful. It glistens in the moonlight.
You flow like an angel as you dance before me.
Forever I will love you. Forever I will caress you.
Forever I will protect you."*

The little girl and the king were married and lived happily ever after. And this is how the little girl became the queen of the king's heart.

This story is a direct parallel of how the Lord's unconditional love changes all of us into beautiful princesses that are being prepared to become His bride. Together we will spend eternity with Him and live happily ever after.

You did it: you changed wild lament into whirling dance;

You ripped off my black mourning band and decked me with wildflowers.

I'm about to burst with song; I can't keep quiet about you.

God, my God, I can't thank you enough.
PSALM 30:11-12 (THE MESSAGE)

The ladies in that conference became that little girl in the story. The love song in the story healed all of their deepest hurts.

GOD HEALS EVERY PAIN

In another country the girls leading the worship had never practiced together. They were the worship leaders from three different churches. The Spirit of the Lord fell and the girls began singing a song from the Spirit of God. Everyone had their part of the song. It was so powerful that all of the ladies that did not believe in the power of God sat there like they had seen a ghost. The song was the prayers of the ladies in the night. They fell to their knees and began to worship and cry out to God. It was a personal visitation from God to prove He listens to their prayers. I cried all day and into the night. God knows exactly what we need and when we need it.

I think the most powerful conference we had was when one of our team members, Judy Stokes, taught on alcoholism. She and her husband both were alcoholics many years ago.

We listened to a secular song called, "The Little Girl Behind the Couch." When I heard it I cried my eyes out. The song was about a little girl whose father was an alcoholic. He was abusive to her mom when he came home drunk, and the little girl would hide behind the couch. Judy said that alcoholism has left a mark on everyone who has an alcoholic member of their family.

There was such an anointing on her class everywhere that we went. My team of teachers were crying their hearts out. The ladies would come up and tell about the person whose drinking problems they had covered up for years. When they told it they were talking from deep within because it was a secret that had been kept for many years. They were finally able to get it out and God began healing them from all of their hurt and pain. Judy hugged one lady who collapsed in her arms. The presence of the Lord was so heavy that the lady just laid in her arms for the longest time.

We taught the same subjects in every country, but in every country the message came out totally different. I think they drew on the Holy Ghost and He ministered to the particular needs of the ladies in each conference.

In another conference we taught about "What To Do When Your Teenager Comes Home Pregnant." The teachers were David and Jody Baker. David is the founder of ten churches. His parents and Jody's parents were missionaries for many years. I was so impressed at how they handled the situation with their children.

FOOTSTEPS OF FAITH

A seasoned pastor's wife came up to be prayed for. She had thirteen children. Only three of the children were girls. Two of the three got pregnant outside of wedlock. It devastated her. To make matters worse, the children were not born normal. The pastor's wife was ashamed of her daughters and pretty much disowned the grandchildren.

The Bakers shared about how they dealt with it when their kids came home pregnant. The whole conference was on forgiveness and standing by your daughter to draw her close to God in order to be restored. We have all made mistakes. The pastor's wife was able to release all of that anger and guilt and shame, and she is a new person today and a very loving grandmother. Little by little God has healed the grandchildren who were born with disabilities.

When pastors' children come home pregnant, the parents have a lot more to deal with than regular parents. Many times the people in the church reject them. Some leave the church.

One pastor said he was so ashamed of his daughter that he made her get up in front of the church and confess her sin. After she did, he called the church to shun her for the whole nine months of her pregnancy. Even in the home no one talked to her or had anything to do with her until the baby was born. The pastor wanted to make sure that the congregation realized that his daughter was the one who had sinned and she should be punished for it. This conference, of course, really caused them to see what a horrible mistake they had made. That night they went home and apologized to their daughter, and God began to heal their relationship. The pastor told his church that he was wrong and apologized. He asked them to forgive him and not to shun his daughter any longer. The baby was born and has been such a joy to the whole family. So many lives have been changed through the conferences.

The late Dr. Lester Sumrall once said that pastors' wives were the most miserable people that he knew. I found that to be true over the years in all of the countries in Central and South America. The pastor pretty much is loved and appreciated. They hold him in high honor, but she is treated like a thing that just came along with the package. Many wives feel God has called them to do something, but they are never allowed to bloom in that area. It is a pretty macho society. The men rule their women with an iron hand.

I was in Guatemala one time and the pastor called me into his office after the conference. He said to me, "Jeanne, we want to withdraw our invitation to you to have these conferences for pastors' wives." I remained silent until he was through talking. He said that the pastors in Guatemala want to keep their women in submission because their main purpose in life was to have children and to serve their husbands. The pastors did not want that to change. They did not want the wives exposed to any Western ideas.

This particular pastor did not like the changes that he had seen in his wife. I asked him what the changes were. We have really been careful not to present anything that would encourage women's liberation. He said his wife was so happy and full of joy, and he did not like that change. He had met with several other pastors and they all agreed that there had been some life-changing in their wives. None of them liked the changes. One pastor remarked that his wife thought she had personal worth and value, and he did not like that.

I agreed not to come again. I was never so grieved for pastors' wives in that country as I was that day. God knows, however, and He will reach them and speak into their lives in another way. He hears their cries for purpose in life.

In 2007 I quit having conferences for pastors' wives in other countries. That season in my life had come to an end. The Lord told me to put my full efforts in the Darien. I began having the conferences there.

ERECTING A RADIO STATION

In 1997 the Lord spoke to Dennis's heart about erecting a Christian radio station. Everyone that he talked to laughed at him. They would do everything to discourage him. He would hear comments like, "You want to erect a Christian radio station in the densest jungle of the world? I hope you have a lot of money." So Dennis always told everyone that his father owned all of the cattle on a thousand hills. Many people thought his dad lived in Texas and raised cattle for a living!

In Panama the government controls all of the radio frequencies. They would not sell us a frequency, but a national radio station in the city told us that we could broadcast from their frequency in the jungle. So we came under their frequency and Esterio Vida 105.1 Darien was birthed. They have been a tremendous blessing to us over the years.

FOOTSTEPS OF FAITH

We still work hand in hand with them in a lot of events.

The engineers told us that we had to buy the highest mountain in the jungle to erect a 100-foot tower in order to reach the whole jungle with our signal. So we went house to house and bought the top of the mountain. It cost us $3,000 and we had to make up sixteen different contracts for the people who owned the land.

After we bought the land we began to do the legal work. It took us four years to get all of the correct papers to raise the first tower. We had to have all kinds of environmental studies done to see how this tower would affect the mosquitoes and monkeys, etc. It is hard to do things legally in Panama because the government is so corrupt. If you do things legally it costs you double the money and it takes a lot longer. Dennis is a real stickler on integrity and he insisted on paying the extra to make sure everything was done legally. It doesn't pay to start cutting corners because of money. But they really do make it hard to do things legally. One man told us if we wanted to do it legally that meant that we had to pay for his signature, which had to be on the final papers. He charged us $2,300 to put his signature on the approval of the papers. It made us mad, but we wanted it to be legal.

Finally we got all of the signatures and papers done, and then the engineer changed his mind as to where the tower should be erected. He said it would be better if we erected a tower on our mission complex. So we put up a 100-foot tower next to the radio station building. It turned out to be a blessing because it is so convenient!

On February 8, 2001, we went on the air and it has raised a standard of the Word of God in the jungle that is hard to measure.

The first thing that Dennis did was to put a two-year Bible school over the air. So many of the young pastors had shared with Dennis that their hearts' desire was to go to Bible school.

140

Almost none of them had any Bible training. The Bible school trained all of the national pastors in the Word of God.

Since this was the only Bible training that they had, it brought so much unity between the denominations. Basically everyone believes in a good God. But people now know the difference between whether God sent a trial or if it is from the devil. Before, they blamed everything on God. Now they realize that God does not send trials to teach you things. There is no darkness in Him. It is the devil that comes to rob, kill and destroy.

This is when miracles began to manifest in all of the churches in the jungle. The people in the jungle believe the Word of God. There are not many doctors in the jungle. You believe God or you die. They believe that God is always with them and when they cry out to Him, He is always there for them.

Dennis also put a Bible reading program on the radio in which the Bible was read out loud twice a day since many people in the jungle are illiterate.

In the jungle there are not many telephones, so we put a program over the radio that allowed the people to send messages to one another. This became one of the only ways people could communicate with their families who did not live in the same area. For example, if Alberto Cabazon was in the hospital they could send a message saying, "Will the family of Alberto Cabazon come to the hospital in Santé Fe? Your father has had an accident and is not expected to live."

Because of this service every person in the jungle owns a radio. It is the first thing that is turned on in the morning and the last thing that is turned off at night. At that time the radio coverage reached a 40-mile range. People who lived farther than that said they were miraculously receiving the radio signal.

At this particular time the police were having a major problem with the anti-government guerilla groups coming over the Panamanian and Colombian borders. They lived in the jungles because it was almost impossible for them to be tracked. They would cross over the borders to kill and rob in order to supply their soldiers. They were heavily armed and seemed to not have a conscience.

The police began training young soldiers to guard the borders of Panama and Colombia. The chief of police came to Dennis and told him that he had a problem with these young soldiers committing suicide. He asked Dennis what he should do. The police chief is a very strong Christian. We agreed together for the money to buy each soldier a

personal Bible. Dennis told him the only thing that could stop the suicides was the Word of God.

So the police chief went back and made it mandatory for every police station to listen to our radio broadcast. No other radio station would be allowed even on their private time. This solved his problem. He said his men are brave soldiers today and they have never had a suicide since he made that order!

Pastors from everywhere traveled for days in order to come to the radio station. They would spend a whole day talking to Dennis and getting counseling.

Truck drivers would stop in at the radio station and thank Dennis for the station. They always had the same testimony. They would say, "My whole family is Christian, but God is working on me. I listen to this radio station every day. God is planting seeds in my life and one day I will make Him my God."

We went back to the United States to raise money to keep the radio station fully functioning. The electric bill alone was $500 a month. The equipment was very expensive.

ANOTHER ANTENNA?

The Lord spoke to Dennis's heart about erecting another antenna that would cover the whole area of Darien and into the red zone areas of Colombia. There are no churches in that area. Nothing is allowed there. The new antenna and tower would reach 70,000 people on a daily basis.

We shared our need for the new antenna while in the States. One church donated the entire amount. I think it was a God-ordained vision. We have never had one church donate that kind of money! We estimated it would cost $120,000. When all was said and done, we had $148,000. In less than one year every dime came in. That is the Body of Christ working together to fulfill the vision of God.

Every year we have an anniversary celebration at the mission property. We have 68 acres and we clear off about five acres for the big celebration. Every one looks forward to it. It is like a county fair! People come from everywhere to participate in it. All of the churches help with the celebration. Fifty churches were involved in the last one we had.

We always run the celebration live over the radio. This particular celebration was overwhelming. The first night there were maybe 200 people that came. We bought food for 800, so we were fine. The second night 3,000 came. Ha! We were totally not prepared! So the next morning we ran out and killed a cow, 16 chickens and a pig. The third night 5,000 came! No one was mad. Everyone went to nearby stores and bought bread. That is one thing I love about the people here. They are very forgiving and truly believe that you tried your best.

On the last night of the celebration a young preacher preached on the walls of Jericho. He said, "When I get to the seventh time around the wall I want everyone to shout the name of Jesus."

On the fifth time around, all of the men in the crowd fell to their knees crying out to God. There is just something so special to see men drop to their knees in adoration to God. There was such a tangible presence of God and all of His holiness.

The seventh time around the wall the people screamed, "Jesus!" When they did that it was like the power of God exploded all over the crowd. You could hear a pin drop. No babies cried; no toddlers were acting up. A young teen of fourteen years who was born blind started screaming, "I can see!" For lack of better words it was like lightning fell from the sky. The power swept through the crowd and many were healed. Many flooded the altar and gave their lives back to God. Many children received the Lord in their lives along with adults.

This awesome power went over the radio and more than 70,000 people felt that power. They traveled for days to the radio station giving testimonies. A lot of unbelievers came to see the teenager that was born blind who could now see. His testimony went on for months.

Words cannot explain the incredible tool that the radio is for preaching the gospel. Everyone calls it their radio station!

MORE MIRACLES

Once while we were gone to the United States, a young daughter of a female pastor friend of ours was going to school in Panama City and an insect bit her. It caused her brain to swell. She was mentally insane and was in the hospital for three months.

When we came back from the States they told us of the situation. We went immediately back into town and sat with the pastor. She was exhausted. She had been sleeping on a folding chair next to her daughter's bed for three months.

When you asked the young girl something she would get a sick smile on her face and quote scripture. She would never answer your question, but always quoted the Bible and never the same verse. Her mother obviously had taught her the Bible very well. It was all that came out of the child's mouth.

We gave the pastor the book, "Christ the Healer." She read the book and told the doctor that she would be taking her child home. The doctor agreed because he said they could not do any more for her anyway and it was best that she die at home. There were five children bitten by the insect and they still had not been able to identify it. The doctor told the mother that the other four were mentally ill with no chance of returning to a normal life. She told the doctor that was not going to happen to her daughter. The mother and daughter went home. The mother took authority over the devil and began calling her daughter back into her right mind. Within two weeks the girl was completely normal. She went on to study in the university and made very high grades!

There was another lady who gave birth to her fourth child. When the baby was born she noticed his eyes were closed. The skin was covering them and there was no opening in his eyelids. The doctor told her that he was not blind and if the skin was not covering his eyes he could see. She placed her hands on his eyes and prayed for the little boy. When she was done she took her hands off of his eyes, and the skin was in her hands. His eyes were opened and normal!

We had a little baby born with a breathing problem. When the baby was 24 hours old he could hardly breathe. He kept fighting for every breath. His mom walked to the nearest clinic, which was 15 miles away. The doctors checked him over and all five gave the same report: "Ma'am, you better go home and dig a hole because your baby is not going to live. He has one deformed lung and the other one is full of disease." She ran out screaming , "No!"

She ran to her pastor's house, which was eight miles away. "Pastor," she said, "come quickly. The doctors say the baby is going to die!" They ran eight miles back to the clinic.

When they arrived the doctors said, "We are so sorry but while you were gone your baby died. His little body is lying over there wrapped in linen." They do not embalm the dead here, so they bury them within 24 hours.

The pastor said it was like something hit him in the stomach. He could hardly contain the compassion of the Lord for this little baby. He went over and took the child in his arms and put him next to his chest. He began groaning in the Holy Ghost. He said it was like rivers of water going round and round on the inside of him. He saw the compassion go out of him and enter into the mouth of the baby. The baby had been dead for three hours, but started crying. The doctors said, "Take the linen off of the child. He is alive!"

The doctors were licensed to practice medicine, but they asked her to take the baby into Panama City for tests to make sure he was okay. The pastor told them that he would go along and testify about what had happened. When she got there the baby was tested and the doctors on the Board of Medicine called the clinic doctors in to give an account of what happened. The head doctor asked, "Why did you all sign a false death certificate? This child has been tested and there is absolutely nothing wrong with him. He is one hundred percent healthy!"

The pastor began to give his eyewitness account of what had happened, especially how the compassion of God had healed the baby. The doctors on the Board of Medicine looked at him and dismissed the case! They wrote in the medical journal: "Baby was alive. Baby died. Baby is alive now from UNKNOWN sources."

CONFERENCES IN THE JUNGLE

We began having conferences in the jungle for pastors and their wives. These conferences changed the lives of so many pastors and their families. We brought in a couple of guest speakers from the United States. The conferences would last for three days. The guest speakers taught from 9 a.m. until 2 p.m. every day and then at night we would have open-air crusades for the public.

Over the years we have had so many miracles in these conferences that it was hard to record them all, but I would like to share a few with you.

A lady pastor had an incurable blood disease. She was six months pregnant and the doctors told her that she had given this disease to her unborn child. They were going to give her a blood transfusion but they were pretty certain that it would kill the baby. The pastor came to one of the conferences and was instantly healed! She went for her regular checkup and they told her that they could not find any disease anywhere in her blood.

Another lady was pregnant with her 13th child. The baby was in the process of aborting when the doctors told the family that she would probably die during the natural process. She came to one of the conferences. She did lose the baby, but she did not die. Today she is healthy and whole.

A young pastor named Luis was with his dad and they were building a pigpen. His dad told him to be careful with the nails because it was very hard wood. About that time a nail ricocheted and went through Luis's iris. The ambulance rushed him to Panama City with the nail in his eye. They operated but the doctor said he would never see out of that eye. Luis told the Lord, "I can't preach with just one eye." He sees in that eye today!

Not too long after that the whole village was out cutting coconuts. They climbed a 40-foot tree, cut the vines, and the coconuts fell to the ground. They put the coconuts on a table and whacked the shells off with their machetes. A pastor whacked the shell of one of the coconuts and the man standing next to them had his finger on the table. He severed the man's finger totally off. It was lying on the table. The pastor told him not to worry because God would heal him. He tied a dirty white rag around his finger and they worked three more days in the jungle harvesting the coconuts. It never bled or had pain in it. When he got home his wife asked what was wrong with his finger. She was a Christian but he was not. He told her the story. She could see a scar all the way around the

finger. She convinced him to go to the clinic and have it checked out. The doctors were so fascinated by it that they sent him into Panama City. The medical doctors there studied his finger. They could see that the finger had been totally severed, but they had never seen a finger cut through all the nerves and tendons and have a person still have the use of the finger. He could move it and use it as normal. He explained that the pastor told him not to worry about it because God would heal it. They wrote it up in the medical journals as an unexplainable mystery!

ONE-NIGHT CRUSADE

In the jungle you cannot fail at anything because you are the only thing going on, so everyone comes from miles away to anything you have.

One time we held a one-night crusade and about 500 people came from everywhere. There were so many people there that we took the walls of the church off so everyone could feel a part of the crusade. We had a seasoned pastor, Arnoldo Gutierrez, in from Arizona. He was raised in Mexico.

The Indians really know how to worship, and they were deep into worship when all of the children got up and began to dance. They danced and danced and then they fell out in the Holy Ghost. The presence of God was

so strong that you seemed to be in a cloud where His glory was poured out.

A young teenage girl about 14 years old rose to her feet and began to dance. She captivated everyone. She danced like she had taken ballerina lessons her whole life. I have never seen anyone dance in the spirit like that. There was a silence over the entire crowd; then she fell out in the Holy Ghost.

Pastor Gutierrez went over to a young boy on the front bench. He reached out to the boy and said, "Come run with me." Everyone in the crowd gasped because that little boy had never walked a day in his life. He had just had his fifth operation and the doctors told his mom they could not do any more and the boy would never walk. The little boy grabbed the pastor's hand and he ran all over the church. He was instantly healed! Today he is on a soccer team.

About that time the young teenage girl asked if she could give a testimony. She said she was born with epilepsy. She never could run and play with the other children or go to school because she had so many seizures. She told us that Jesus had come to her that night and asked, "Can I have this dance?" She danced with Jesus, and she knew He had healed her. She has never had a seizure since. She later married and had two children.

CHAD'S MOTORCYCLE

About this time Chad had a bad motorcycle accident. One of his friends came running up the lane crying, "Mrs. Cook, come quickly! Chad is lying in the ditch. He has had an accident." I drove down about a mile from the house and there was Chad lying next to his bike in the ditch. He was unconscious. We put him in the jeep and rushed to the clinic. The doctor said, "Chad is in a comma. He probably will not come out of it because he has a very severe head injury. It looks like he has broken his back, his kidneys have been bruised, and it looks like he has broken his arm and elbow. But do not worry. Since he is your son, I know he will be okay!" That doctor had seen so many miracles that were just unexplainable. However, he sent a nurse with us to Panama City and said if he vomited blood he may never recover. Chad vomited all the way in to Panama City (10 hours).

When we got there we went to the emergency room. There was another couple there who had a son who had the same kind of accident. Almost identical. The doctor was not a Christian. He checked Chad out and told us, "If he does not wake up in three days, he never will. Even if he does, he will not know you. Your son died tonight. He will be a vegetable because his head injuries were so severe. He broke his hip and bruised his kidneys severely. He broke his arm and crushed his elbow." There was such a grace on us that we just sat there in complete peace. Dennis replied to the doctor, "You will see. He will walk out of here." The doctor yelled at us, "Don't you understand how severely your son was hurt tonight?"

We were there three days and nights and Chad was still unconscious. On the fourth morning he opened up his eyes and said, "Mom, I am starving!" He walked out of that hospital with a severe concussion so he had to be careful not to have a head injury for five years. He did not break his hip, but he did crush his elbow. He did not know what had happened until about one year later when he remembered. Basically he just lost control of the bike. He did not remember hitting anything. He was very afraid to get back on the bike but Dennis encouraged him to overcome the fear or he would never overcome it. He had to face the fear to conquer it. He did and rode the bike several times after that.

THE BRIDGE TO PUERTO LARA

Dennis had a pastor and his bodyguard in to preach in Puerto Lara. It was rainy season and the road usually becomes very slippery. There are drop-offs on both sides of the road. Dennis drove over a bridge which was two large trees thrown across the riverbed. It was about eight feet high. When he went across, one of the men said he heard a big crack.

FOOTSTEPS OF FAITH

Dennis went on into the village and held an evangelistic conference. After the conference he started going home. The road had grown worse because the rain had not stopped. When he started to cross the bridge he told the men to hold on tight. He got about halfway over the bridge and the front wheel got stuck in a hole in one of the trees. Dennis put it in reverse, thinking he could just pop it out of the hole. Keep in mind he only had an inch on each side of the tires! About that time the back of the truck fell off of the bridge, but thank God, the axle held the truck on the bridge. Dennis walked back to the village and the Indians came and pushed the truck backwards until it was off of the bridge. They filled in the hole with rocks and dirt. Dennis tried again. No one would ride with him. They thought he was nuts, and he was! He got stuck in the hole again. So they pushed it back off of the bridge one more time.

There was another way across the river...through the river. By this time of night it was very dark. Dennis went down the hill and into the river to cross it and got stuck in the mud. So they dug the truck out again. Dennis got the speed up and gunned it. He got almost out but hit a tree he didn't see that was in the water. So they pushed him out of the river. This time they packed the tree with mud and rocks so when he would hit it the speed would throw him up onto the bank of the river. When he was going really fast and hit the tree, he went airborne. They had to push him the rest of the way up the hill, but they all got out safely that night!

HEARTBREAK IN LOS MONOS

We had a wonderful crusade for three days. Many people were healed and born again. I have gotten really close with the children in the villages. In this particular village a little boy named Ronnie sat on my lap for the entire crusade. He is the little boy second from the left in the picture. He reminded me so much of one of my own grandchildren back in the United States. I treasured that moment so much. It filled a void inside of me because being away from grandchildren is my greatest sacrifice. I have known this little boy his whole life. He grew up in Sunday school. His mom and dad were very strong Christians. His dad was an elder in the church and on many occasions traveled with us visiting the churches. Ronnie was 5 years old then. I loved him so much.

The next morning I took some things to the village. Everyone was very sad and acting very weird. I asked them what was wrong. They said little Ronnie had died in the night and his dad buried him that morning. Dennis was so angry because it is not normal for a child to be healthy one day and die the next.

It is the law in Panama that when a child dies an autopsy is done to see what was the cause of death. Dennis asked Ronnie's dad why he buried him so quickly and did not obey the law. He was emotionless and just looked at Dennis. The Bible says that the eyes are a candle into the soul. Something did not set right in Dennis, but he let it go.

One week later Ronnie's little 18-month-old brother died. Dennis demanded that they take him to the clinic to see what was going on. When they did the autopsy, they found that he had died from starvation which was caused by a worm that enters into the body through the heel of the foot. It is usually found where there is chicken or other bird feces. The worm eats everything that the child takes into his body. That is why they look healthy, but all the time a worm is slowly killing them. The doctor said that it was possible that Ronnie died of the same thing.

After their deaths their dad turned into a different person. We had never seen this side of him. The spirit of discernment was trying to tell us something, but we just could not figure out what it was. He was highly respected and had been faithful to the church for years.

One day soon after that, the children were playing with the keys to the church and the keys got lost. The pastor's wife went house to house asking the children if they had the keys or if they knew what happened to them. At the first house she went to, the 9-year-old girl started crying. The pastor's wife had a tender heart for children. She told her it was okay because they would find the keys.

The little girl cried even harder and said, "You know, right, what happens in the church?" The pastor's wife did not know, so the little girl went on to say, "Ronnie's dad sexually molested me there." The pastor's wife said, "No, honey, I did not know that. I am so sorry. I promise I will make sure he will never bother you again."

When the wife told the pastor, he was in shock. The pastor's wife thought there was more to the story, so she went from house to house asking the children for the keys. Nine of the children (boys and girls) confessed they had been molested in the church by Ronnie's dad.

In the Indian villages they solve everything by voting. They have a village meeting and the whole village is required to be there. They heard the case and the chief asked some pretty blunt questions. He asked each child if they were given something to perform the sexual act. Each child said that they had been given a dollar. So the chief asked if they were aware of what it meant when they received the money and the children all said yes. Then he asked if they enjoyed what he did to them and they all said yes.

The village voted and said that the children could have said no because they were fully aware of what was going on and he did not force himself on any of them. He was released and let go free from all charges. When Dennis heard it he was so angry. The Panamanian law has no jurisdiction in the Indian village. The Indians take care of everything that goes on inside of the village unless someone files a complaint with the Panamanian law.

Dennis talked to the church. "Someone needs to stand up against this attack on the church. No one can tell me that man did not take advantage of a child 9 years old by giving him or her a dollar." So he convinced them to file a complaint with the Panamanian authorities. They tried him and found him guilty. He went to prison for three years in a very horrible prison.

When the man got out of prison, he asked to come back to the church. We counseled the pastor that he could come back but he could never be seen with any children. The man refused to obey the conditions. He said that the church had done him wrong. The only reason he had done those things was because he was taking drugs. The drugs made him do it. Dennis told him he didn't care what his excuse was and that he must obey the conditions. He refused and never came back to the church.

That was the hardest thing that ever happened to me in the ministry. I grieved over those little children for the longest time. Even as I am writing this I am crying. It just affected me so deeply. I did not think I would ever get rid of that pain.

Then on top of it, I was so disappointed in myself for not seeing the signs in Ronnie's father. I started studying on how to recognize child molesters and how to know if you have one in your church. We had never dealt with something like that before and never have since. He had every sign but we were just ignorant and did not recognize them.

We learned a lot through this situation. We also began teaching hard on the importance of wearing shoes. Most of the kids in the villages wear shoes now. Ministry life has many unspeakable joys and many heartaches. You have to learn to give it to the Lord and trust Him to be able to get you over it.

THE BODY OF CHRIST IN ACTION

We have had many different kinds of groups over the years come here to minister, and it has been a great blessing. It is beautiful to see the Body of Christ helping each other in whatever the needs of the missionary might be.

The most popular groups are the youth groups. We thoroughly enjoy working with teenagers. They have brought many blessings into our ministry. The thing that I love the most about teen groups is their witness to our teens. Our teens look at American kids as having everything and yet they love God. It speaks very loudly to them. We have hands-on outreach for the teens. The youth teach an already prepared curriculum. I write the curriculums that they teach. I always make one around the needs of that village at that time. They are responsible to lead their group to the Lord, to water baptize them, and also to pray for them if they are sick. The teens leave totally changed. They feel like they are very important to God. They prayed for the sick and they were healed. They preached the gospel and people got born again. They water baptized their disciples. They get very close to the people in their group. It is a wonderful experience for them. They leave having paid a high price to preach the gospel...living in grass huts for a week and bathing in the dirty rivers as well as having to use incredible outhouses. All of these adjustments seem to be a life-changing experience for them!

Once we had a large group come in from Rhema Bible School. Dennis and I both graduated from Rhema's two-year school in 1980.

FOOTSTEPS OF FAITH

There were 50 students on the team. I divided the team up and sent 10 into each village.

Dennis took a team of 10 to Rio Cito where we have a church. It is ten and a half hours by canoe. The loggers had just opened up a new road but, because the dry season was about to end, I asked Dennis not to go on the virgin road since it had never been traveled before. I was concerned because of the rain. There would be no way out if the rains began. That area is dense jungle, and tigers and everything else roam around there!

It was in this village that Dennis was going to teach the Indians about the Holy Spirit. When he got there they were all speaking in other tongues! He asked them what was going on. An older lady said, "We don't know! A strong wind blew in the hut and we have been speaking a weird language ever since." Dennis then spent time explaining to them what had happened. He was pretty excited!

Back at the house I realized that the team had left the food for the whole trip behind. There are no places to buy food that deep in. I prayed about it and God told me not to worry, so I just got busy assisting the other groups.

The night before Dennis and the team were to leave Rio Cito, the rains began. It rained all night. I knew they were in trouble so we all agreed in prayer that God would protect them and get them out of the jungle safely. Dennis said the road was solid mud and they were slipping all over everywhere. They came upon a hill that they had to climb, so they hooked the winch up to a large tree. When the winch began pulling, it brought the tree to them instead of pulling them to the tree. So they hooked it to another tree and, little by little, they were able to winch

themselves up the hill. They got going really fast because of the mud and then hit something in the road. It jolted everyone, and someone caught one of the team member's foot right before he fell under the tire of the truck.

I went to meet them, praying all the

way that they would make it out safely. Here they came. The brown truck looked like red clay. The dirt here is red clay dirt. I have seen the truck really muddy before but this gave a different meaning to dirty! I brought everyone a cold soda. No one was talking. They were covered in mud.

Since it was dry season we had to ration the water. Normally you could only use two gallons to clean up in. That night we all made an exception to the rule for them. They were still very quiet and did not want to talk about it.

The next day you could not shut them up. They laughed and laughed at everything that they had been through! They told a story that Dennis told them not to eat snacks unless they ate the whole thing because of rats. One of the team members had eaten some cheese crackers but fell asleep before he finished them. They had draped mosquito nets from the rafters to keep rodents and bugs that might fall off the thatched roof from getting in or under their sleeping bags. During the night the team member was awakened by something running all over inside his sleeping area. When he caught sight of it, he yelled out for help. Instead of his team members helping him get rid of the rat, they were making sure the rat could not get into their sleeping area. Somehow the rat got out and left the area. No loyalty on that team!

We have had many groups in over the years and they have been such a blessing to us.

In between groups, we hold special conferences for the pastors and their wives every three months. We bring in seasoned pastors from the United States to share in the classes. In this culture, people who are seasoned in the ministry are highly respected.

I have a meeting with some of the regional directors of different denominations and ask them what they need help in. Then I plan a conference to teach on those areas. They are all full of the Bible but very few have any experience in how to handle the practical things in the ministry. We teach on things that no one else touches on. We do a lot of sharing  of personal situations in our lives and things we learned over the years. It is like older men and women teaching younger ones how to minister to people in a more effective way. The pastors and their wives love the conferences and look forward to them. We are still holding conferences today.

This ended the last season of this book. I pray you have been blessed by our experiences and have enjoyed seeing how God has moved in the lives of the Indians in the Darien Jungle. I plan on writing another book in the future taking off where this one ended.

ABOUT THE AUTHOR

Jeanne and her husband Dennis have four children who were raised in the jungles of Panama. She home-schooled all four children through the 12th grade.

Upon graduating from college in the United States, two of the children settled there and the other two live in the jungles with Jeanne and Dennis and work in the ministry. The two in the United States are also very active in Vida Ministries.

Jeanne attended Rhema Bible Training Center in 1979-80. In November of 1981 she and her husband and their four children, ages 8 to 12, moved to Panama to work in a leper colony. Two years later they pioneered a work with the Chocó Indians in the Darien Jungle of Panama.

The radio station, Radio Vida 105.1, was established February 8, 2001. Its signal reaches an estimated 70,000 people every day. It is the only Christian radio station whose signal goes into the drug farms of Colombia. It also reaches the entire province of Darien which is the largest province in Panama. One of the programs broadcast over the radio is a 2-year Bible school. Most of the pastors in the Darien have completed this Bible school.

Jeanne is the executive vice president and administrator of Vida Ministries. In addition to running the day-to-day operations of the ministry, she travels throughout Central and South America holding conferences exclusively for pastors' wives. She also founded a children's ministry in the jungles of Darien to educate the children in the Word of God. Along with these responsibilities, Jeanne teaches at conferences for women and married couples.

Vida Ministries, Inc.
PO Box 6433
Lafayette, Indiana 47903-6433
E-mail: jeanne.vidamin@gmail.com
Web Site: www.vidaministries.com